Bittersweet Memories

The Life Story of an Immigrant Daughter

BARBARA HUSSMANN LONG

Bittersweet Memories

The Life Story of an Immigrant Daughter

Barbara Hussmann Long

ISBN (Print Edition): 978-1-54397-587-1

ISBN (eBook Edition): 978-1-54397-588-8

For My Family

"There are two lasting gifts we can give our children, roots and wings."

~ Goethe

PREFACE

Bittersweet Memories is the memoir of an immigrant scientist daughter's journey from despair to hope. It is a story of survival and growth. She is transplanted to America, and her new life is fraught with painful circumstances. Isolation, divorce, and mental illness impact her formative years. The challenges of life in a new country reveal the best and worst of human nature. With fear her constant companion, carried by forces within and beyond herself, she kept going with unwavering determination.

Her childhood home was like that of a Grimm Brothers' tale, shrouded in a mysterious aura. She was seen as pretty, polite, and different, but people never really knew her. Her experiences were almost make-believe, but they were real. One may wonder how and why it happened, as she does. Through it all, she comes to realize that everyone struggles, but that they can choose their own future. She carries with her the belief that she will become stronger and wiser. It is hoped that in her story, others may find support and encouragement to get them through their own difficult times.

1. MEMORIES

I knelt beside my father's grave in Germany as the sun was setting. It was Sunday afternoon, the flower shops along the boulevard were closed, and I regretted I had nothing to leave behind. While reaching into my purse for a tissue to wipe my tears, I pulled out my business card. On the back of it I wrote "Dear Father, I'm sorry we didn't get to know each other, there was so much I wanted to say."

After tucking the note into the shrub next to the headstone, I walked away, recalling the last time I saw my father at age eighteen. He had come to the restaurant where I worked, with hopes of talking with me. My heart beat as I saw him get out of his car. In disbelief, I noticed that my mother-- they had divorced when I was eight years old—was seated at the far end of the dining room.

Not knowing what to do, I hid in the kitchen. My mother had forbidden any contact with him, and by now, her control over me was nearly total. My father realized I wasn't coming out, and left. I had not seen or spoken to my father since I was ten. He left the restaurant without even nodding to my mother. It would be eleven years later that I received word of his death. There was so much to explain, and now that couldn't happen.

It was a cruel twist of fate. What if she had not been in the restaurant? Should I have talked with him or called him later? But this was a father I hardly knew. What I did that day can only be understood by those who have fallen under the power of fear. For years afterward I looked for him in every red car.

In my search to learn about my father, my husband and I made a trip to Germany, now with our little girls. In Munich my father's German childhood friend and colleague, accompanied us to my father's grave. After lighting a candle, and wiping away tears, I asked his colleague if my father understood the reason why I rejected him was fear of my mother's retaliation. "No, he never understood," was his reply. It was then I knew I had to tell this story.

I was in kindergarten when my mother, brother and I were shopping. Waiting in the car I heard someone tapping on the window. It was my father. He had seen me sitting there from the window of his consulting office, while my mother was across the street at a convenience store. I slowly rolled down the window, and watched anxiously to see if my mother was coming. He leaned down and through the open window said, "Your mother is not well, she is imagining things." I started crying. At five years old I was trying to absorb what was happening.

I didn't want to believe what he said, yet I knew there were problems at home. My brother had started sleeping in my mother's bedroom, while my father slept in his room. I tried to understand what he was saying, but was attached to and also fearful of my mother. "You have to believe me," he continued, "it is not your fault or your brother's." What was going on, I thought, as my father's words echoed in my mind? I wiped away tears as Mom returned to the car, never knowing what happened.

Meanwhile, my brother's life had grown bleak. Blackie, our dog, and my brother's best friend, was taken to a dog pound. A neighbor had reported my family as being immigrants, and immigrants were not allowed to keep a dog according to an outdated law. Such distrust was similar to life in Nazi times, which our family had just left. Broken-hearted, my brother sobbed, and said "why did we have to come to America?"

I dreaded the days and nights of quarreling and fighting. My mother endlessly accused my brother of minor issues. A workman, doing repairs on the furnace, apparently dropped a cigar on the basement floor. My brother was accused of intentionally putting it there to upset our mother that someone entered our house. This became the "cigar story" as my brother and I tried to figure out what was going on. Obsessions over what most people considered minor incidents continued and increased.

As tensions grew, I hid under the staircase in the basement. My arms and legs felt heavy as that of an elephant. My brother, only eleven years old, thought if he confessed to things he hadn't done, everything would be alright. It didn't work. Mom continued to accuse him, he grew nervous and started to stutter. Years of writing letters of appeasement passed, in a vain attempt to lessen her outbreaks.

Before he left for college, my brother's final coerced letter revealed he was still under her spell: *To Whom It May Concern: I hereby affirm that any letters or confessions I have written are the complete truth. I have written these letters in full seriousness, and still have the opinions that I set forth in them.* A sense of unworthiness and pain continued most of his life. Fortunately for me, I must have remembered what my father tried tell me many years before.

While clearing out my mother's house, I found my favorite childhood book "Of Courage and Valor," biographies of famous men and women. It had been one of my father's last gifts to me. While leafing through the book, a yellowed piece of paper fell out. It was a letter my brother had written to me that I never received. Broken-hearted, I recalled his unhappy youth that he expressed in the letter. In it he tried to say he didn't deserve Mom's accusations, especially the names he had been called by her: liar, traitor, devil, evil, Lausbube, and that he belonged in a reform school. My brother couldn't tell anyone because, as a teenager, who would have believed him. Despite his efforts to appease, he was told that fate would punish him. Little did we know how fate would take a tragic turn.

When World War II ended, Germany was in ruins. My father, a German engineer, was among a select group of scientists mandated by the United States government to come to America. This became known as "Operation Paperclip." Its purpose was to secure high-caliber scientists in strategic fields. It was apparent the US and USSR were ending their war-time alliance, and that the Cold War was beginning. Germany had designed and built the V-2 rocket, the world's first guided ballistic missile. Its power was from the use of liquid nitrogen and alcohol. Since it flew faster than the speed of sound, it could not be heard before it struck.

From "American Raiders: The Race to Capture the Luftwaffe's Secrets": *Revolutionary developments in aeronautical engineering were in progress in Germany a long time before we fired our first shot against the Nazis. Yet, a long time after that shot, after we had managed with considerable difficulty to gain the upper hand over our enemies, there we were, out in no-man's-land, scrambling around for the secrets of Nazi airpower. We hadn't listened to the foreign correspondents who told us in newspapers, magazines, and books that Germany was working on something big.*

Technical power was important to both former allies, and the rush was on to recruit German scientists. It was likened to that of a treasure hunt. The scientists selected were "superlative specialists" and would save the US years of work and billions of dollars. Other German scientists were not as lucky as they and their families were transported to small villages where there were neither research facilities nor work. There they were interrogated until the Office of Military Government of the United States was satisfied that all desired intelligence information had been extracted from the scientists. It is estimated that 1,800 technicians and scientists, plus 3,700 family members were part of this group. They were detained for month's even years in an effort to deny German reconstruction.

My father had never belonged to the Nazi party, and clearance was quickly granted. His departure, January 1947, on a troop transport ship to New York was swift. My mother found herself alone with both grandmothers, my five-year-old brother, and herself three months pregnant. They all lived in a small apartment outside of Frankfurt. Both my grandfathers had died young.

While crossing the Atlantic Ocean, he wrote in his journal: *After seventeen days of enduring heavy storms at sea, the sky darkened, the sun and its red light vanished and all the hundred thousand lights of Manhattan appeared. I stood on the deck admiring the impressive sight, and talked with an American officer about my future in the United States.* Prior to his undergraduate and doctoral studies, my father had thirteen years of schooling including five years of English instruction. His knowledge of the English language would prove to be a great asset in coming to America.

While they leaned against the ship railing, an officer told my father about the Statue of Liberty as they passed her in the harbor. It had been designed and built in France in 1884 and shipped to New York, a gift from France to America for its principles of liberty. The base of the statue was funded by ordinary adults and children. The well-known words engraved on the pedestal were written by Emma Lazarus, a Jewish young woman:

> *A mighty woman with a torch, whose flame*
> *Is the imprisoned lightning, and her name*
> *Mother of Exiles. From her beacon-hand*
> *Glows world-wide welcome; her mild eyes command*
> *the air-bridged harbor that twin cities frame.*
> *"Keep ancient lands, your storied pomp!" cries she*
> *with silent lips. "Give me your tired, your poor,*
> *Your huddled masses yearning to breathe free,*
> *The wretched refuse of your teeming shore.*
> *Send these, the homeless, tempest-tossed to me,*
> *I lift my lamp beside the golden door!*

My father's assignment was to Wright-Patterson Air Force Base in Dayton, Ohio. Operation LUSTY (LUftwaffe Secret TechnologY), as the mission was referred to, was the United States Army and Air Forces' effort to capture and evaluate German aeronautical technology after World War II. They acquired 16,280 items to be examined by intelligence personnel who then selected 2,398 items for technical analysis at Wright Field. My father's group of eighty-six German scientists included aeronautical engineers who developed the world's first jet-powered fighter, and now were needed for technical analysis.

Rocket-powered jet aircrafts were pioneered in Germany. The turbojet was invented in the 1930s, by a British physicist, and later Hans von Ohain, a German physicist. Soon afterward Germany's aero-engine manufacturers were urged to begin jet engine development, and a contract was given to *Junkers* Motorenwerke. However, when the Nazis came into power in 1933 they requested its founder, Hugo Junkers, come to the aid of German rearmament, he declined.

Nazis responded to his defying of orders by demanding ownership of all patents and market shares. This included the threat of imprisonment on the grounds of High Treason. In 1934 Junkers was placed under house arrest, and died having to give up the remaining stock and interests in his company. Against the wishes of its director at BMW in Munich, where my father was employed, they now where required to concentrate on aircraft production, and automobile manufacturing stopped altogether.

My father was later relocated to Klöckner-Humboldt-Deutz, an aircraft manufacturer. In 1940 their diesel research division was relocated to Oberursel, a suburb of Frankfurt, where my godfather led the development of larger and more advanced engines for aircrafts. There they worked on the 16-cylinder, two cycle diesel engine. However, work was halted in late 1945 after the factory was captured by the Allies and turned into a tank repair depot.

Just like my father, Hans von Ohain, a German scientist, came to the United States under Operation Paperclip for research also at Wright-Patterson Air Force Base. Nine years later, he became the Director of the Air Force Aeronautical Research Laboratory, and by 1975 was Chief Scientist of the Aero-Propulsion Laboratory at Wright Field in Dayton, Ohio.

Wright-Patterson was central to ensuring the German equipment, documents, blueprints, and detailed drawings were properly housed as well as analyzed. An Air Force report concluded that the technical knowledge gained here would revolutionize American air power. However, it was reported that some of these scientists were treated not much better than prisoners, even receiving rations of food, and needing special permission to travel.

Designations about Project Paperclip at times differed between the Justice and State Departments. German scientists at Wright Field, and other places, were sometimes called enemy aliens, though the program had been a sanctioned under President Truman. The administration concluded: *The value of this presidentially approved program to the nation as well as to the naval and military services warrants full support of the War Department.*

There were limited quotas for those entering the United States, and some Jewish groups were rightly concerned that Project Paperclip might allow *Wissenschaftlers*, German scientists, to immigrate and become American citizens without thorough background checks. America, Russia, Britain, and France all wanted these scientists and their knowledge. Some groups didn't understand, or didn't want to understand, how important these specialists were to our nation and its security.

Operation Paperclip ended in part when West Germany protested that its scientific expertise was being drastically depleted. By 1948 a German economist described the loss of brain power as almost fatal to their nation. He went on to state "The scientists and engineers whose education was the product of centuries of cultural revolution are scattered to the four corners of the globe. History alone can tell what fruits this transplanting of German genius to foreign soil will bear." The German scientists who came to the United States, and became American citizens, such as my father, helped shape their newly adopted country, as many immigrants had done, in this case in the fields of science and technology.

The Project Paperclip name was derived from Army Ordinance officers' practice of attaching a paperclip to the folders of scientists they wished to employ. The paperclip signaled to investigators that they should expedite the background check. The program officially concluded September 1947. By 1949 the Commerce Department had placed the Paperclip scientists at three educational institutions, Cornell University, Penn State University, and North Carolina State College. They also went to companies such as RCA, Bausch & Lomb, AVCO, North American Aviation, and Dow Chemical. Ninety percent of the scientists who arrived between 1945 and 1947 remained in America and became naturalized citizens. Once it became clear that the "Paperclippers" were permanent employees, not glorified POW's, both the civilian and military sectors paid them what they were worth.

Wernher von Braun was the most well-known of the German Paperclip scientists, an aerospace engineer and space pioneer. My father and von Braun attended the Technical University of Berlin at the same time, both in the department of mechanical engineering. Von Braun went on to become the leading figure in the development of rocket technology. In America he worked for the United States Army in the intermediate-range ballistic missile program, and developed rockets that launched the United States' first space satellite, and eventual journey to the moon.

From an account in the 2018 book by Brian Crim: "Our Germans: Project Paperclip and the National Security State" *The MIC (Military-Industrial Complex) of the Cold War period owed much to the previous German accomplishments, and with the US acquisition of 1,500 scientists and technicians in the decade after World War II, Germans put their indelible stamp on America's greatest scientific endeavors of the second half of the twentieth century.*

Along with a bound copy of my father's doctoral dissertation, I have his leather flying helmet. During the early years of aviation test pilots wore these helmets as a form of protection from the noise and cold. Both of these are treasured reminders of how my father's skills were highly regarded in Germany, known for its world-class scientists and inventors, and also in America.

Coming to America is a popular song by one of my favorite singer/ songwriters, Neil Diamond. It speaks of the dreams and aspirations of many in making their way to this country.

Far--We've been traveling far
Without a home
But not without a star
Free--Only want to be free
We huddle close
Hang on to a dream
On the boats and on the planes
They're coming to America
Never looking back again
They're coming to America

The song is optimistic about immigration and the great possibilities of this country. During my teenage years, I sometimes had mixed feelings that perhaps my father had somehow betrayed his homeland. He had a family to support, a future to consider, and democratic ideals that beaconed. He was among the many immigrant creators who have added to this country since its beginning:

Alexander Graham Bell, Scotland, Inventor of the telephone
Andrew Carnegie, Scotland, Steel manufacturer
James Gamble & William Procter, Ireland & England, Procter & Gamble
Joseph Pulitzer, Hungary, Journalist
Irving Berlin, Russian, Composer
John James Audubon, Haiti, Naturalist
Thomas Mann, Germany, Novelist

Albert Einstein, Germany, Physicist

Ellie Wiesel, Romania, Author

Elizabeth Taylor, England, Actress

John Lennon, England, Musician

Sergey Brin, Russia, Google co-founder

Daniel Aaron, Germany, Comcast co-founder

2. BACKGROUNDS

It took a year and a half before my mother, brother, and I received clearance, after my father left, to come to America. During the period of my father's absence, my godfather, watched over our family. Both he and my mother had been accomplished pianists, and often spent afternoons playing duets. It was not long after we settled in America, that we received the terrible news he had taken his life.

At the end of World War II, my godfather had told the Army and Air Force he was willing to come to the United States with his engine designs to continue research and development. It was not to be. Younger scientists were chosen as opposed to those of more senior status, and the invitation never came. In a letter to my father he wrote "Perhaps after all, an opportunity will come to us who are left behind with broken wings." Instead, he watched as his life work was demolished before his eyes with the coming of the Allied forces.

Germany was devastated, and many of my godfather's colleagues were either in the US or Russia. My father and he had patented a diesel engine that my father sold to an American firm. My mother insisted, a few months before my godfather's untimely death, that my father obtain a contract for the sale of the patents, insuring he'd receive payment. My father went on to patent further inventions relating to internal combustion engines. As an employee of the United States, however, these were for the sole use and purpose of the government, without payment or royalty. It too saved the United States untold funds.

That winter living conditions in Germany were grievous. Because my father was now employed by the US government, my mother received additional rations. However, the process took months while our family hungered, like much of the country. Dependents of these scientists were then entitled to twelve hundred grams of fat per month, as opposed to three hundred grams for every other German. She also received twice as much bread and sugar per week, seven rather than two eggs per month per person, and three times as much meat and more than twice as much cheese and jam.

Once families were relocated to the temporary housing for Project Paperclip at Landshut, a town in Bavaria in the south-east of Germany, they were allowed two pairs of resoled shoes per family per year. Those living outside of the compound were allotted one pair of resoled shoes. Not every family of the selected scientists would eventually immigrate to America.

The war had forced my maternal grandmother to close the hotel that she and my grandfather had owned and operated in the spa resort town of Bad Munster. Their first hotel was in Siegen, where my mother was born, and was one of the largest hotels there. Prior to having children, they had taken an around-the-world voyage. This grandfather, whom I never knew, had an unquenchable thirst for culture. He was kind, fun loving, and gregarious, to whom I owe personal traits.

My grandmother woke early on Christmas morning, 1944 with an ominous feeling. She had declined my parent's invitation to leave the hotel as she knew homes that stood empty were plundered. A bridge not far from hotel had already been bombed and rebuilt numerous times by then. Because it was off-season, no guests were in the hotel as she hurriedly made her way to the neighbor's house, moments before the bomb hit.

The force of the blast threw her to the ground. Although rattled and bruised, she survived. Allied pilots weren't supposed to bomb small towns; however, bridges were a prime target for the transport of troops and supplies. The bombs missed the bridge and hit the hotel. A second bomb fell on the bridge the day after Christmas. March 1945 the bridge was destroyed by the German Wehrmacht to prevent the Allied troops from making their way to Berlin, capital of the Reich.

My parents took my grandmother to their apartment where she remained throughout the war. The hotel could have been repaired, but all able-bodied men were in the war. Those who were not enlisted were builders who were needed to repair hospitals and bridges. In this resort town over seven hundred residents lost their lives to the bombing of the bridges. During this time able-bodied women and children cleared the rubble from the bombed spa treatment center in town, and it was rebuilt. A plaque at the bridge citing these details stands as a reminder of the insanity of war.

The years of war affected my mother's health. She was exhausted, and under-nourished as rations from the German government were sparse, and even the US government allotments were limited. Four months before I was born, the grandmothers pooled their resources to make reservations at a resort for my mother and brother to recuperate. Spa hotels were issued greater amounts of rationed food.

Not much was working after the war, including the once efficient trains, their tracks having been bombed. The booked resort town was close to the Polish border. There were ample reasons for Polish people to dislike Germans by this time, and that day the train was occupied by many Polish immigrants. It had been scheduled to arrive at the resort town the same day, yet for unknown reasons sat idle on a track through the night. My mother, conspicuously pregnant, was called a baby killer, among other accusations. Terrified, my brother hid under a seat of the train.

It was a ghastly night as many German passengers were accosted. When the train finally arrived, she was gravely ill and was transported to a nearby hospital, also in disrepair. What had been thought to be exhaustion was an infection of her lymph glands. The doctors were overworked, and paid little attention. Knowing she was very sick, she instructed my terrified five-year-old brother what he should do in case she died.

He was not allowed to stay at the hospital, but slept by himself at the hotel, making his way everyday across the fields with his knapsack filled with provisions. I later found photos taken of him forlornly walking to the hospital. This heart-rending situation, and the war in general left deep impressions on my brother that time wouldn't fully erase.

After her conversation with my brother, my Mom telephoned the nearest US Military base, informing them of her plight, and her husband's status with the US Military government. Instantly she had the chief of surgery at her bedside, and an operating room was prepared. There she was told she'd survive only if the baby she was carrying was aborted. Paper work was telegraphed to my father, to be signed for an abortion. He signed, agreeing to it if his wife would not otherwise survive. Thankfully that didn't happen, and I was born. My father's acceptance to work for the US military turned out to be life-altering. If my mother hadn't been able to appeal to the US government for help during her illness, both she and I might not have survived.

On a hot July day, my mother was in labor as a taxi took her and her mother to a hospital near Frankfort. I arrived into this world healthy and well, though we stayed longer than usual so that she could regain her strength. In the absence of my father, my godfather was a frequent visitor to the hospital. When she and I were discharged, the nurse predicted I would become a source of joy and happiness.

The taxi made its way back to the apartment as she rested her head on the seat and thought of her time as a young woman in Florence, Italy. *On a sunny afternoon as she walked across the Duomo Square, a Gypsy woman ran up to her, tugging at her sleeve. The Gypsy said that she had an important vision of my mother's future. She predicted that my mother would marry a man with blond hair and blue-eyes, in contrast to her black hair and green eyes. The marriage would fail, she was told, leaving two children, one bringing grief and the other joy.*

We were dropped off at the apartment, her daily routine resumed, and the vision became a memory, but still one that she'd revisit as time passed. The grandmothers were worried and depressed from the war, not knowing what would happen to them. My mom's solution in dealing with the myriad of daily details was to place me in a carriage on the veranda. This continued through the fall and winter until the day I was forgotten, and snow gathered on the top of my carriage.

The grandmothers were preoccupied with what to feed the family while my mother searched in town for US government rationed food. Unlike many babies, I did not contract rickets, the disease caused by lack of calcium and vitamin D. My daily dose of fresh air and sunshine spared me, and also kept me out of the chaos of the home. Soon, however, we were required to house a refugee family in the already crammed apartment. The struggle continued.

Similarly during the French occupation in World War I, a regiment of troops took over my grandparent's hotel consigning the family to a couple of rooms. In the evenings, they were seated at their dining room table while upstairs the soldiers frolicked to music. The ceiling lamp often fell to the table from the vibrations, my grandfather shaking his fist in the air. They had to watch helplessly as their damask tablecloths and bed linens were shredded and used to clean their rifles, then thrown out the windows to hang from tree branches. Through all of this, my grandfather's hair turned white, prior to his stroke.

In Hamburg, wealthy family friends had their villa occupied by British forces. They were ordered to leave in two hours, taking only what they could carry. They bribed the soldiers to allow them to go back to retrieve valuable possessions. When allowed to return permanently, after the occupation, the house had been completely looted, even by their countryman. The lady of the house died soon afterward in a car accident, and her husband succumbed from grief and failing health.

Near the end of World War I, in my family's neighboring town of Bad Kreuznach, the main spa hotel became the temporary headquarters of Kaiser Wilhelm, the eldest grandson of Queen Victoria. During this time, the Kaiser, along with President Paul von Hindenburg and General Erich Ludendorff met for talks in the area. Ludendorff visited with guests at my grandparents' hotel, and my family often saw Kaiser Wilhelm and Hindenburg. Later, by the time Hitler came to power, Ludendorff was no longer sympathetic to him.

In January 1933, Hitler was appointed Chancellor by President Hindenburg, and Ludendorff sent a telegram to Hindenburg: *I solemnly prophesy that this accursed man will cast our Reich into the abyss and bring our nation to inconceivable misery. Future generations will damn you in your grave for what you have done.* This may seem eerily parallel to events in our own time. We may hope that those who remember history will not repeat it.

A devastating winter flood of 1917 damaged the Kaiser's headquarters, and the offices were moved to the Belgium town of Spa. Before Hindenburg left the area, local schools were closed in his honor. His parting words to the crowd were, *don't forget your spirit.* November 1918, Hindenburg's replacement, General Wilhelm Groener, traveled to meet with Kaiser Wilhelm in Spa. It was there Hindenburg bowed in submission, and let the newcomer Groener take over.

Kaiser Wilhelm remained stoic to his final days. In Berlin, Prince Max von Baden proclaimed Germany as a socialist republic. The new Germany had no room for an emperor, or Kaiser. On November 10, 1918 Kaiser Wilhelm, the last German emperor, was dethroned. The five-hundred-year rule of the Hohenzollern dynasty was over. In exile now, Wilhelm fled to the Netherlands, never again to step onto German soil. The following day the armistice was signed effective six hours later. The war was over. As the masses convened in Berlin, the removal of Kaiser Wilhelm was officially announced, as well as the renunciation of Crown Prince Wilhelm, the Kaiser's eldest of six sons and would-be heir to the throne.

Interestingly, my father's godson, a movie producer in Berlin, made a movie about Kaiser Wilhelm's life in exile entitled "The Exception," starring Christopher Plummer and Lily James. The connection between Kaiser Wilhelm's life and that of my mother and grandmother during this time was fascinating to me. The movie also depicts the Jewish underground movement and its redeeming efforts during those tumultuous years.

To better understand my mother, I needed to consider her background. As a young person, she was vivacious and well-liked. Her dream was to become a doctor, not the care-taker of a small hotel. This was not to be as her father lay paralyzed, and she was needed to help. During the sixteen years my grandfather lived after his stroke, he was taken to an assisted living facility each year when guests arrived at the hotel. At the end of the season, he'd return again. The rental of his room, when he was gone, helped defray the costs of his care. Even my mom's room was rented as it had a beautiful view of the Rhinegragenstein. This rock formation towered above the river and was the highest north of the Alps. At the very top of rock, the ruins of a castle built in 1050 was a popular attraction.

The town has another attraction, the largest open air inhalatorium in all of Europe. Tall wooden structures are used for the production of salt, removing water from the saline solution. The Nahe river valley has numerous salt springs and for two-hundred-seventy years salt has been extracted from the springs. Large wooden water wheels push water to the top of the towers for gradual evaporation. The towers consist of wooden wall-like frames filled with bundles of brush and thrones. In total, the graduation towers are slightly longer than a football field in length, and have a surface area of over 8,000 square meters. As the saline water trickles and evaporates, it creates a fresh microclimate like that of a seaside town. Park benches line the sidewalk alongside the towers as people breath in the healing properties of the air.

With youthful determination Mom walked down the street to the hotel, seeing it through the eyes of a prospective guest. She made a momentous decision that if she couldn't leave for a career, she would turn the hotel into a well-respected and popular destination. Her newly constructed flower gardens and walkways gave the grounds an appealing look. A new promotional brochure was made where she irritated the town officials by placing a picture of the hotel closer to that of the famous rock.

Into this quaint spa town, like many, a Hitler Youth Group was forming for boys and girls ages fourteen to eighteen. The girls club was called the League of German Girls. A close neighbor was an organizer of the emerging Nazi Party in 1933. He summoned my mother to come to his office where she was appalled to see her name listed as a leader of the local girls' club. In revolt she crossed her name off, and left abruptly. It was apparent to her that even then something terrible was happening in Germany.

When she came home, her father, in a trembling voice, said tomorrow they'd come for her. She knew this was a real possibility, as a local teacher who had joked about the Nazi movement suddenly disappeared. The local organizer carefully erased her name, but not without the warning she'd pay for her refusal. Thus, began an era of fear and suspicion, not only for the country, but for her.

3. DARKENING CLOUDS

Following World War I many political organizations were forming, all wanting to assume leadership in Germany after the war. The young fanatic Adolf Hitler was leader of the German Workers' Party founded in 1919 in Bavaria. In 1920 he renamed it the Nazi Party, and the same year, directed the formation of the Youth League of the National Socialist Workers' Party under the leadership of storm troopers known as the SA, or Sturmabteilung.

In March 1922, an official Nazi newspaper proclaimed: *We demand that the National Socialist Youth, and all other young Germans, irrespective of class or occupation, between fourteen and eighteen years of age, whose hearts are affected by the suffering and hardships afflicting the Fatherland, and who later desire to join the ranks of the fighters against the Jewish enemy, the sole originator of our present shame and suffering, enter the Youth League of the National Socialist German Workers' Party."* The rules included: "*love of one's country and people; enjoyment of honest open combat and healthy physical activity; the veneration of ethical and spiritual values; and the rejection of those values originating from Jewry.* That May in Munich, the Nazis held their first meeting at a beer hall, to announce the foundation of the Youth League. Only seventeen attended.

Munich, in the state of Bavaria, was a base for the Nazis as well as other groups who opposed the democratic government, the Weimar Republic, which was centered in Berlin. By November 1923, the Nazis, who now numbered in the tens of thousands, attempted to overthrow the elected government in Bavaria in the famous Beer Hall Putsch. For this uprising, Hitler was tried and sentenced to two years in the Spandau Prison. It was during this time that he wrote his deep grievances, with the assistance of Rudolph Hess, in the book "Mein Kampf."

The global Depression of the 1920s and 1930s was more severe in Germany then in the United States and other countries. Rebuilding from the previous war, and paying debts and reparations, took its toll on finances and people. Stories of wheelbarrows full of Deutsche Mark to buy groceries were not far from the facts. A loaf of bread at that time cost 1000 Deutsche Mark, or the equivalent of $1350. My mother's violin cost a small fortune in devalued money.

My grandfather died in the spring of 1935. No longer needed for special care, my mother took trips during the off-season. She was hired as an au pair for a wealthy family in Florence, Italy, where she was accepted and appreciated. The following year she traveled to Berlin for dietician school. There my father was a doctoral student at the Technical University, a most prestigious institution, especially in my father's field of mechanical engineering. My father completed his doctorate in 1937. During his college years, he and a best friend used to buy both liberal and conservative newspapers, exchanging them while sitting on a park bench, a show of open-mindedness and objectivity. My parents began their relationship, amid the darkening clouds of their country and the world.

At the 1936 Berlin Summer Olympics my mother boldly made her way, without a ticket, to the reserved seating area of the new Sports Stadium. As the guard requested her ticket, she fumbled in her purse pretending to have one, when just then someone called her name. It was a former hotel guest, and a high-ranking military officer. The guard staunchly saluted, and she was seated in the reserved section, surprisingly not far from Hitler's boxed seat, catching a glimpse of him.

Hitler had built a new 100,000-seat track and field stadium, as well as six gymnasiums and other smaller arenas, and the games were the first to have radio broadcasts, reaching 41 countries. Hitler's plan was to surpass the Los Angeles Olympics of 1932. This would be the last year both Games were held in the same country. During the Olympic Games, and with pressure from the Olympic committee for "fair play," the Nazi regime attempted to downplay its military presence. Hitler ordered anti-Jewish signs to be taken down temporarily. Nazi deceptions were not totally successful as Western journalists reported troop maneuvers during the Olympics. To the Fuhrer's consternation, the African American sprinter Jesse Owens won the Gold Medal that year.

Winter Games were held that same year in the town of Garmisch-Partenkirchen in Bavaria, where America's Sonja Henie won her third consecutive gold medal for figure skating. She became one of the highest paid Hollywood stars of the 1940's. Controversy stirred when Henie greeted Hitler with a Nazi salute at the Olympics, and after the games she was invited by Hitler to his vacation home in nearby Berchtesgarten, where he gave her an inscribed photo of himself.

During my parents' time off, they took trips together. Both liked to ski and made plans to go to St. Moritz, Switzerland. On the fourth day of their vacation, they joined a group that was going high into the Bernina Ranges, the mountains between Switzerland and Italy. It took hours to reach the bottom of the mountain, and my mother skied down a slope beyond her skill and fell, splintering her leg. Initially she was cared for at a small Alpine hospital. Then it was discovered the leg had been improperly set, and she was moved to a hospital in Munich. At the hospital in Munich, my father visited her regularly during her four months of convalescing.

While boarding the train to Munich, an SS officer noticed my mother on crutches, and offered to pay for a first-class compartment, in which he had a reserved seat. Conversation ensued and he spoke of Hitler in glowing terms. She asked how he knew so much about this new leader, and he replied that he was one of the early lieutenants and had even received bullets meant for Hitler.

From Wikipedia about this SS officer: "After his studies Graf joined the Bavarian Army. He resigned the army in 1904 after he was wounded and became town clerk in Munich. During the First World War he became a member of the German Worker's Party and was a founding member of the Sturmabteilung SA. In 1921 he became member number 2882 of the NSDAP, National Socialist German Workers Party."

"Graf was an amateur wrestler and a butcher's apprentice, and became Hitler's personal bodyguard from 1920 to 1923. He was present at the Beer Hall Putsch, where, with Rudolph Hess, he cleared Hitler's way to the platform. During the subsequent march through Munich, Hitler, Erich Ludendorff, and their followers were blocked by about hundred-armed police outside the *Feldherrnhalle*. Graf stepped forward and shouted "Don't shoot! His excellency Ludendorff is coming." There was nevertheless gunfire, and fourteen Nazis and four police officers were killed. Graf shielded Hitler with his body, received several bullet wounds, and possibly saved Hitler's life. Graf recovered, and rejoined the Nazi Party after Hitler was freed from prison. By the time Hitler came to power, he was a *Sturmbannfuhrer* in Heinrich Himmler's SS, equivalent to a Major in the Wehrmacht."

"In December 1924 Graf was elected Councilor in Munich. In that same year he rejoined the forbidden, newly founded NSADP as member # 8. From the end of 1925 he was assessor of the NSDAP supreme court of justice. He was re-elected as Councilor in 1929. In 1937, he was promoted to the rank of SS-*Oberfuhrer* and on 20 April 1943, Hitler's birthday, became an SS-*Brigadefuhrer*. On Graf's birthday, 3 July 1943, he received a book from Himmler, thanking Graf for saving Hitler's life 20 years earlier. In 1948, Graf was sentenced to five years hard labor and died in March 1950."

To this man, Mom sent as a gift wine from her hometown, and a thank you letter to which he replied. In the letter he indicated that normally he couldn't accept gifts but rules have exceptions. He wrote he'd like to visit her hometown if ever in the Rhine country. I have the original letter of May 2, 1939, and under his signature the title *des Fuhrers alter Begleiter,* the Fuhrers old companion. I don't know if he ever visited, but we do know the rest of the story, on September 1, 1939 World War II began.

The stage was set for my parents' life together when he asked her to marry him, and she accepted. It was a beautiful late May Day in 1939 for an out-of-town wedding on the Tegernsee. Guests were arriving at the lakeside hotel near Munich. At my mother's home, the hotel guests were also coming for the season. My strong-willed grandmother insisted on an out-of-town wedding with only closest friends and family. This was a disappointment to my mother as she had always dreamed of a big wedding in her home town. After the ceremony they were to be driven in a chauffeured car intended for only the bride and groom. Instead she had to ride in a city bus to the reception, while the guests rode in the limousine. As she sat in the bus in her black and white wedding gown, my mother felt, despite the sunny day, a dark cloud hung over her.

Upon receiving his PhD in 1937, my father rented an elegant apartment on a prominent boulevard in Munich. In the same building lived a Jewish family who sensed the impending doom, and had tickets to flee Germany. Since my parents were setting up a home, they bought from this family their household furniture, including a Steinway grand piano. In the rush of circumstances, the family was relieved to have a buyer, they left quickly, and were not heard of again.

Meanwhile radio was coming of age in Europe, enabling the Nazis and giving Hitler a bigger audience. Publicity was placed in the hands of Joseph Goebbels, Minister of Propaganda, and he made cheap radios available to the public. By 1938 Germans were thoroughly familiar with Hitler's spectacular public appearances. There were even signs of Fuhrer fatigue, from his barking, staccato speech, interspersed with cheers and Heil Hitlers. In America it must have seemed bizarre to radio listeners when their regular music programs were interrupted by an announcer stating they were going live to Berlin. Back in the homeland, the Nazis made it a treasonable offense to listen to oversees radio. Anyone caught doing so faced time in a concentration camp, and by the first year of the war many Germans were imprisoned for listening to London-based broadcasts. My parents kept a radio hidden in the attic, and when everyone was asleep, they'd listen quietly to overseas broadcasts. Everyday life changed as the war advanced and America entered the conflict in December 1941.

The war was relentless, and speeding up production took precedence over everything else. Many German engineers, including my father, were soon aware of the absurdity of the war, and in secret delayed requests and plans in order to slow production. If found out, this could have cost them their lives. However, the move to a suburb of Frankfurt was a saving grace, as six weeks later their apartment building in Munich was hit by an incendiary bomb, and destroyed. The new tenants of their vacated apartment had their previous home damaged by a bomb, and now were homeless again. From the outskirts of the city they could see Frankfurt burning, and air raids seemed to be getting closer.

People were instructed to hang dark curtains from windows, and sirens gave warning of approaching strikes. In some cases, they fled to the basement, while gates were left open for neighbors to seek shelter. Even in such dire circumstances humor was a cherished part of life. One of the tenants in my parent's apartment building owned a parrot, and during the raids, as bombs fell, the parrot screeched, *Actung! Actung! Uncle Albert!* But this was serious. At the end of the war it was discovered why parts of the city were spared, a POW camp for downed Allied airmen was located in the vicinity.

As the end of the war approached and enemy soldiers were just outside the town limits where my family lived, all men ages sixteen to sixty were given weapons and ordered to dig trenches for the defense of the city. Women, children, and the aged were commanded to evacuate. My mother remained, thinking it better to die at home than on an unknown road. The city was shelled for two more days until a clergyman, seeing the futility of continuing the war, raised a white flag of surrender just before the Allied Forces were about to attack.

At last the war ended, and American and other occupying forces streamed in on tanks and truck convoys. My brother sat on a curb along with other children begging for chewing gum and chocolates, from the soldiers. He had never had chocolate candy or chewing gum before.

4. ANOTHER COUNTRY

On a hot day in July, my mother, brother and I boarded a US Liberty Ship in Bremerhaven bound for America. My seven-year-old brother was not allowed to share a room with us instead slept in a dormitory with returning US soldiers. He was scared about the two-week voyage, yet tried to be brave. When news came about atrocities that occurred under the Nazis, Germans became suspect, and were despised. I cringe to think of the taunts he might have received, and the terror of being separated from his mother and me.

Food on the ship was plentiful, but we fell ill. Ice cream would have been special, but it was too much for our stomachs that hadn't had rich foods for so long. While crossing the Atlantic I turned one, and my brother tearfully asked who would take care of his little mimosa tree, when he realized we were not going home.

Our journey to America was under US Military auspices, and my father greeted us at a Navy port of Hoboken, NJ. To his disappointment, I cried when I was placed in his arms, the first time he had ever seen me. His five-year assignment after Wright Field was at North Carolina State College in Raleigh, North Carolina, but due to a polio outbreak we were flown to Rochester, NY instead. It was arranged for us to live with a German Jewish family for three months. Though my parents were sympathetic to all Jews, their bitterness toward them was understandable. Our transition to America was not going to be easy.

Diesel engineering in Germany was more advanced than any other country. North Carolina State College had the main diesel school in the US at that time. Five thousand-pound crates including the Braun cathode-ray oscilloscope, were shipped from German laboratories, for his analysis at the college's research lab.

The early years in the South were surprisingly carefree. Both German and English came naturally for me, but my brother missed his grandmothers and friends, even his mimosa tree. He spoke English reluctantly, though he often practiced next to my crib. Entering school, he was required to speak English, but wouldn't. His resistance was so bad that my mother resorted to tricking him. She told him that an immigration officer was going to send him back to Germany if he didn't speak English. He finally complied, under this threat.

At a Fourth of July fireworks display, he bragged to his friends that in Germany he got to see fireworks for free almost every night. He was referring to planes that sent sixty flares which then floated to the ground, each burning for many minutes. These markers for Allied bombing raids were called "Christmas trees."

Obscure German folklore and superstitions were a part of our upbringing. Like most three-year olds, I liked to dance in front of our full-length mirror, until a blanket covered it, and I was sternly told that a devil resided within the mirror. I thus stayed as far away from mirrors of any kind. Most boys of seven resist cleaning their rooms, yet my brother was coerced by Mom as she tapped at his bedroom window with a pronged clothes line stick, reminding him to get busy. It took years before he questioned where the stick's mouth was. Tricking him into submission became a pattern for my mother.

Mom was often overwhelmed with the many changes in coming to America, and I was left to play on my own in the townhouse complex. I made friends easily including the neighbor girl with whom I conversed in German enough so that she repeated German words, to the astonishment of her parents. I was also self-sufficient enough that when thirsty in the summer I'd push aside flies in a bowl meant for the pet turtle, and drink the water. These years were comparatively good for both of us, and my brother eventually made friends with other German scientists' children.

At an early age I noticed something was not quite right with Mom. She'd carefully study my German Kate Kruse doll saying that someone was intentionally damaging her face. In reality, as a toddler, I had tried to wash off the bright red rouge that was on her face. Even then I kept quiet, so she would not become upset and angry with me.

My mother's command of the language, even after five years of English instruction in German schools, was broken. She found herself the object of ridicule on numerous occasions as she struggled with pronunciations. She frequented one local meat market in particular. On her first Easter in America, she planned a festive meal of roast duck. Going to the counter she told the grocer, "Please, I want to buy a dog." The grocer replied, "Sorry, lady, we don't sell dogs here." She responded, "But my friend just bought a dog here." The butcher did not reply, and she went on, "Let me explain, I want a dog that can swim, you must understand," she continued, "I want a dog that lays eggs." By now people were gathering and laughing, including the employees. Though dog and duck sound alike they are not the same. Humiliated, she walked out and never returned, homesickness set in again.

Nevertheless, she tried to assimilate as best she could. When some of her Southern neighbors said, come and visit sometime, she mistakenly thought they actually meant it. It was an awakening when she realized that this was just a figure of speech, and her company wasn't really expected. While on a summer stroll with the family my mother noticed a boy blowing pink bubbles out of his mouth, and she surmised it was caused by a strange illness. It was her first experience with chewing gum. Although she had never seen a black person before, she identified with African Americans and their plight. The black cleaning lady who worked in our home, even asked to go with us when we moved north. This was not to be.

We made our way to my father's next position in Pennsylvania in our first car, a used Chrysler. After crossing what is known as the Seven

Mountains, near State College, we arrived where my father had accepted a professorship in mechanical engineering at Penn State University, and a partnership with an engineering consulting firm. My mother was pleased as it reminded her of the well-known Seven Hills or *Siebengebirge* of the Rhineland, not far from her hometown. However, the relaxed life of the South came to an end as my mother realized we'd be housesitting in someone else's home.

Her Steinway grand piano was the first shipment to be sent from Germany. Next to arrive were her valuable hand painted Meissen porcelain dishes, started in 1710 in Meissen, near Dresden. They remain one of the most famous porcelain manufacturers throughout the world. To my mother's shocked dismay, many of these antique dishes laid broken in the large drum barrel in which they were packed in-between shredded newspaper. Leaving one world for another was bittersweet.

My father traveled alone to Canada in order to reenter the US legally now as a permanent resident, and be issued a Green Card. This is still the process to become a permanent resident of United States after living in the country for at least five years. With a Green Card one would be afforded all the rights of a citizen, other than not being able to vote. By now, my mother was showing signs of deep mistrust when we did not make this trip across the border together, though we had not resided in the US for five years. Not being able to trust people during the Nazi years in Germany, she may have felt my father and the government had blacklisted her.

It would be two years until she, my brother, and I re-entered the U.S. through Canada. During the trip, with my father along, my brother and I delighted in being sprayed with water on the Maid of the Mist at Niagara Falls. Little did we know that this trip would deepen our mother's illusions when our Green Card had a different status than my father's.

Some of our trips were now taken in secret. One of these was to return to our first home North Carolina. My mother thought that the immigration office there could provide answers for her concerns about the Green Card status. There were no answers, and we began the long drive home. Along the way, we stopped in Washington DC to see yet another immigration lawyer. On the George Washington Memorial Parkway, about to cross the Potomac River, I saw a low flying blimp, and said "Look." Unfortunately, my mother looked, and we crashed into the car ahead of us. Other than a broken headlight and some damage to the other car, we were not hurt. I, however, cried in the back seat as I was blamed for having caused the crash. My mother, unfamiliar with needed papers, didn't have the insurance card. My father was then called to come to Washington.

Queen Elizabeth and Prince Philip were to be in a parade that weekend during their first visit to America. My tears ended as we stood at the side of Pennsylvania Avenue to watch the motorcade pass, and I got to see a real live Queen! I rode with my father as we made the trip back to Pennsylvania, one of the few remembrances I have of him. My brother rode with my mother in her car. I was nervous and excitedly told my father that I had seen my friends in North Carolina. As soon as I said it, I knew I was in trouble. We had been drilled not to say where we had been. When we got home, I quickly went to my hiding place under the staircase.

Our last family trip was to Florida, where my father met with a German scientist who was developing the design for what would be known as the Hovercraft. They worked together for a week while we enjoyed the Florida sun during the Christmas vacation. With childlike excitement my brother and I saw our first alligator! The Hovercraft proposal was not selected, instead an Englishman was awarded the contract three years later.

I was enrolled with thirty-five other children in the Garden of Children, a highly rated nursery school in State College. We were part of the Boomer Generation, I had many friends, mostly children of university professors. Seeking my hiding place was less often, because of the support of the well-trained staff. I was growing into a fairly confident preschooler.

At the age of five, while dining at the Corner Room, a well-known Penn State landmark, I spied a family speaking German and dressed in traditional German costume. Unnoticed by my parents, I hurried over to start a conversation. The family was the famous "Sound of Music" Trapp Family Singers, who were performing at PSU's Rec Hall. After they introduced themselves to my family, they gave us free tickets to the sold-out concert. They also invited us to come to their Inn in Stowe, Vermont, which we did, five years later, then without my father.

5. LIFE GOES ON

My father, the middle son of my grandmother's three boys, received news of his mother's sudden death at the age of seventy-two, just three years after we had come to America. Her oldest son had gone to Brazil during the thirties when Germans were fleeing to South America. From there he helped his family during the war by sending packages of food, even eggs, each one carefully wrapped in newspaper. She never saw him again once the war broke out. Her youngest son studied to be a pharmacist, but when the war broke out, he was called into government service as a foreman in an ammunition's factory. For the safety of his wife and children they lived apart, his family in the countryside. Later he was captured by Allied Forces and imprisoned as a POW.

After the war, all surviving able-bodied men were called to work rebuilding the country. There were few businesses left untouched. He, like my father, had an ability in languages and was sent to Bergen-Belsen, a con-centration camp during the war, now housing displaced persons. During the Nazi era tens of thousands of Jews, Poles, Dutch, Czechs, and Austrians died at this camp. My uncle never got to use his education as a pharmacist, and remained a language teacher until his early death.

In my mother's lucid moments, she yearned for her childhood home and flower gardens in Germany. One night she had a dream of a house in the woods with lots of space for roses and flowering shrubs. In the dream she saw us children playing happily on the lawn, something we could not do in the small apartment we had moved to after house-sitting for a uni-versity professor family.

That summer my brother registered for a week at a YMCA camp, outside State College. The camp had originally been part of the Civilian Conservation Corps, under Franklin Roosevelt's New Deal for unemployed, unmarried men. The idea was to promote environmental conservation, repair, and needed employment. The camp was magic to me though it was only for boys. I loved it, and begged to stay. At the end of the season our family rented the main cottage. I escaped the ongoing arguments of my parents by running through the meadow dreaming I could hear children voices. At night the fireflies entertained me as I danced with them. I didn't know that life would get worse.

During our vacation, and on a drive through the countryside, my mother saw a house like the one she had seen in her dream. The difference was this house was in urgent need of repair. It was far removed from neighbors on a back road. At one time the property belonged to a lumber company, and was used as sleeping quarters for lumberjacks. The well was dry, but there was a water pipe from the mountain, a distance from the house. In the backyard was an outhouse, with two openings on the seat, one for an adult and the other a child.

My mother insisted on purchasing the property, including six acres of woodland, but my father didn't agree. About this time the monies from the sale of the diesel engine design came through. She reminded my father she was the one who insisted he secure a contract for the royalties. The royalty money was then used to buy the house, with the deed in her name. My father, hoping this might appease her, agreed. The marriage was already in trouble.

The property was purchased from a nearby lumberman, who had bought it from the state of Pennsylvania. His sawmill had been purchased prior to the logging company's departure from the area. He was a tough and rugged logger, yet had a gentle side. There was no electricity in his small cabin until neighbors paid for an electric line plus his usage bill. His special skill was to locate water with a dowser. It was here that my mother discovered she had this ability too.

The story went that this lumberman acquired a liking for a local girl in the valley. She, however, had a boyfriend. One evening the lumberman found the young couple in a parked car. A tussle commenced, and the lumberman's revolver went off shooting the girl in the arm. The neighbor destroyed the gun to hide the evidence. Later the lumberman returned the favor to the neighbor's wife while her husband was in jail.

Endless repairs began on what was now Mom's property. A jeep was purchased so that she could drive from town to the country to supervise the workers. Between work visits we had picnics at the Penn Roosevelt Park, also built by the Civilian Conservation Corps. The entire Seven Mountains area had heavily lumbered.

A Penn State extension web-site describes the era:

There were three logging companies that operated in the Seven Mountains area of central Pennsylvania. The men who worked for these companies were tough. They had to be. They worked from sunup to sundown, six days a week. Meals and a bunkhouse were provided by the companies they worked for, and were considered rustic **even by standards** *then. Since OSHA safety guidelines were nonexistent at that time, serious injuries were common. The sawmill operators had the highest turnover rate. If you accidently cut off a critical piece of anatomy, you were out of a job.*

These were tough times in hinterland of Pennsylvania as the story goes:

The Legend of Bunkhouse Bully

Due to the constant close contact and cramped living conditions, personality conflicts were common at campsites. The offended person endured it, beat up on the other fellow, or more commonly, walked off and quit the job. After one such altercation, the man who started the fight disappeared for the remainder of the day. His bunkmates assumed he had quit and gone to town. The following day the cook noticed the well's water pump was jammed. When the cover was removed, they found the missing lumberjack's body, stuffed headfirst into the well.

The lumber era was not to last, as before long many trees were gone. Once the trees disappeared, the people were soon to follow. Lumbermen left behind a barren landscape that would be devastated by erosion and wildfires. The Commonwealth of Pennsylvania bought thousands of acres of deforested land and began the project of reforesting the area.

I often wondered why the pine trees surrounding our house were in straight rows. This was due to the reforesting efforts. By the time we lived there, most of the planted trees were quite tall. Later I'd gather the left-over decaying stumps of the cut trees in winter when we didn't have enough money for coal.

I enjoyed playing during picnics at the Penn Roosevelt Dam, until one day as a typical dreamy six-year-old, I walked off the end of the dock. I panicked while bobbing up and down in the water, my eyes glimpsing the slimy green algae pilings. A fisherman nearby grabbed me. From this experience, fear of being under water remained with me my entire life. I was soon enrolled for swimming lessons in State College. The instructor didn't know of my trauma, and was very strict. I cried every time I was to go for lessons, and refused to continue, or a family crisis may have intervened, and the lessons ended.

6. BREAK UP

Work continued on the property, and Mom used her acquired dowser skills to determine where water was located. Dowsers were known both in German and American folklore as part of a mysterious sixth sense. Meanwhile, I played alone in the woods. My brother was not happy, moving to this new place again meant leaving his friends. Fall was approaching, and we were enrolled in two local one-room schools, one for first to third grade, and the other for fourth to sixth grade.

This time my school was not in a building with bathrooms down the hall. The building had no indoor plumbing, and a pot belly stove for heat in the middle of the room. There was one teacher for twenty-eight students, grades one to three. Some of the students clearly had learning disabilities. Recess was popular as next to the schoolhouse there was a graveyard to roam in. We were primarily on our own, the older students were assigned to watch that we didn't wander onto the nearby road.

During recess, I'd scold older boys for cruelly smothering mice in their field holes, saying "Don't do that, mice have souls too." I was then tied up in a game of cowboys and Indians. I thought I was playing the part of a captured maiden but they intentionally forgot me when the recess bell rang. Their punishment from the teacher was to carry water buckets from the well to the school that day. Feeling vindicated, I skipped with my girlfriends to the nearby country store, and bought my favorite penny candy.

In State College, I had been enrolled in an affluent Presbyterian Church Bible School that taught love and kindness. It therefore came as a shock when the following year, at age six, I attended Bible School in the white clapboard church in the valley, and the theme was not focused on love and kindness. I was frightened by the elder's teaching unless I accepted Jesus I would go to hell. Hell was elaborately shown as a place of unending suffering, something I had already experienced enough of at home.

That summer I had nightmares and couldn't sleep, fearing that the devil, who had been thoroughly described, might be close by. I had heard my mother, during one of her raging episodes, saying she was going to tear off my father's mask and reveal the devil inside. This vivid and scary visualization stayed with me most of my childhood. With time I managed to calm myself by playing house in the woods.

When we moved into the partially remodeled house, it had been vacant for years and everything was moldy and damp, especially the floors. Many of these repairs were hastily done by unskilled workers. The new varnish hadn't adhered properly, and signs of wear appeared sooner than expected. What was a natural occurrence became, once again, a case of vandalism, or intentional damage in my mother's eyes, and my brother the chief suspect. Her anger escalated especially after sleepless nights. I flinched in disbelief when she insisted, he swear to having betrayed her by placing his hand on a Bible.

Christmas season brought out the traditional Advent wreath, German cookies baked and candles lit. It would be the last Christmas my father spent with us. He brought home a large Christmas tree, and I was happy. At the department store I had told Santa what I wanted, a big doll and baby bassinet. Tip-toeing downstairs in the middle of the night, I was overjoyed to see them under the tree. That night I had a sweet dream.

Spring and summer came and went, and now my father only came home late at night, and after we were asleep. On the dining room table, he'd find his dinner menu attached to a ceramic pretzel man. This little figurine now has an honored place beside my dad's portrait and other memories of him. I was entering second grade, still in the one room school house. It was good year, as I had a caring and patient teacher. So different from what I experienced at home, as the marriage deteriorated and fears escalated.

The first winter in our country home brought many new adventures. A snow storm shut us in for a week, with no electricity or water because the pump was an electric pump. Candles were used for reading, and cooking was done on the top of the cast iron stove in our living room. By the fourth day, however, we were out of food. My brother skied to a neighbor's home in the valley that still had phone service and placed an order with the grocer. My mother and I then skied to meet the delivery car, filled our backpacks, and returned on the road covered with snow drifts, some so high a snowplow couldn't get through.

Wind had swept across the valley with such force that on some places you could see the road, while on other spots the drifts were eight feet high. My Dad stayed with a colleague during these storms, waiting until big plows got us out. Schools were of course cancelled. It happened quite often that winter, and for us kids it was sheer pleasure. We were always disappointed when the power lines were repaired, and the electricity came back on.

During Mom's winter driving, we experienced trials and errors, sometimes spinning around in a circle or into a ditch. The uphill road to our house was a particular challenge in maneuvering the curves while maintaining the right speed. I was in the back seat praying, as she accelerated, slipped, and spun her way home. Once we made it to the top I'd proclaim, "My prayers did it again." If we didn't it make it there was always a shovel and a box of cinders in the trunk.

When the wood floors appeared scratched in new places my brother was again implicated. My Dad calmly suggested that his wet ice skates had been left there, but she insisted otherwise, that someone had intentionally done it. He became upset, said she was crazy, and belonged in a mental hospital. They started tussling, his shirt was torn, and she fell down. I was then instructed to take my father by the hand and lead him to the door.

Later she requested that I, a child of seven, write up this incident addressing it "To Whom It May Concern." In bewilderment I looked for hiding places outside the house. During these stressful times my brother's stuttering continued. My mother's mistrust was now directed not only toward my father and brother, but also his colleagues, and even the university. Under this spell, my brother kept lying in hopes of her not raging at us.

Despite the confusion in our lives, I tried to be carefree. Hours were spent playing make-believe in playhouses made of various shipping crates. The bathtub crate became a teepee. The large wooden box from the Steinway piano was turned into a playhouse, complete with windows and a door. My brother painted an unfinished outdoor ping pong table located next to the playhouse. Years of birthday parties were celebrated at this spot. For my first birthday in the woods, unbeknownst to Mom, I had invited the entire twenty-eight students in my school, all three grades, of course not all showed up. But with quick thinking she turned carpenter benches into a base, and plywood planks for the table. Cement blocks and boards became the benches. German children's games were played but not always to the amusement of my classmates. In front of the playhouse was a new rock garden, just like the one in Germany.

We were told about an Amish group that spoke a German dialect. Intrigued, we drove to Big Valley where they lived. Their culture was unique, with no electricity, cars, or phones. Married men wore beards, women plain clothing, and barefoot children played in the fields while older men plowed fields with a team of horses. Mom took photos until she was abruptly stopped by an Amish elder. When he discovered our German was similar to their Palatine German, he softened and became interested in us. We were invited to their church that was held in his home and to lunch afterward.

Our friendship with Amish families continued for years. During a visit, I discovered that a baby lamb's mother had died. The Amish family feared it would not survive as it required frequent bottle feedings. I begged to take the lamb home, and my wish was granted. I even slept with it in the basement until the playhouse was readied. It became the home of my first pet. Shippie grew from a lamb to a ram by the end of summer. My brother and his friends teased him, until they were rammed from behind. We even tried chaining Shippie but he quickly got tangled in the chain. It was touching when Shippie and my brother's Irish setter Misty became best friends.

Soon we realized, however, the time for his departure was near. By early winter, Shippie was taken to a sheep farm. With each visit I realized he was happier with his own kind. The playhouse now had a wood burning stove with pipes through the roof. My mother had dreamed of using it to heat hot chocolate during ice skating parties on the pond. This was a wonderful theory, but never really materialized.

I was fluent in both German and English, and bedtime stories were from German children's books. A favorite of my mom's was "Der Struwwelpeter" or "Sloppy Peter", with its frightening stories written by German psychiatrist Heinrich Hoffmann, and published in 1845. It was filled with tales of misbehaving children, and the gruesome consequences that awaited them. Augustus doesn't eat his soup, and so he wastes away and dies. Harriet plays with matches and sets herself on fire. But none is stranger than the tale of Conrad known as "Suck-A-Thumb:"

> *One day, Mamma said: "Conrad dear,*
> *I must go out and leave you here.*
> *But mind now, Conrad, what I say,*
> *Don't suck your thumb while I'm away.*
> *The great tall tailor always comes*
> *To little boys that suck their thumbs,.*
> *He takes his great sharp scissors out*
> *and cuts their thumbs clean off, and then,*
> *You know, they never grow again."*

Grimm Brother stories like "Little Red Riding Hood" and "Hansel and Gretel" were also read, and were vivid to me because of the rustic life like mine. I still liked stories that told of something better, and how to get there. A favorite American book was "The Magic Key," the story of a brother and sister who had a key that opened to a fairyland. It was like an escape into a happier world. Another tale, "Little Black Sambo," taught that fighting over who is the greatest could turn you into melted butter. I therefore tried to remain humble.

From "Katy and the Big Snow" I discovered the importance of working. Katy the girl bulldozer operator makes a difference in the city of Geopolis. The story "Mike Mulligan and his Steam Shovel," named Mary Anne, emphasized the value of thinking, and that there is always a way out. Mike Mulligan worked hard with his steam shovel, but forgot to make an exit ramp. Never despairing, he becomes the janitor of the new town hall, and his steam shovel the furnace of the building.

My brother was raised with *Max and Moritz* stories. The seven tales of badly-behaved boys was written by Wilhelm Busch, the same time as Dr. Hoffmann's books. The stories begin with two boys tying bread crusts together to trap the widow's chickens. When the chickens eat the crusts and swallow the strings, they become fatally entangled. The boys similarly terrorize a tailor, a teacher, a baker, and farmer. When the farmer notices the boys had cut open his bags of grain, he puts the boys in the bags, sends the bags through a mill, and grinds them into bits. The bits were then eaten by chickens. These kinds of stories were intended to be scare tactics in keeping children obedient.

7. ILLUSIONS

Playing on our property, I discovered what appeared to be quick-sand, and ran to get my mom to inspect the new find. She looked around, warning me not to step into the swampy area. I was then instructed about people being swallowed in quicksand, and thereafter carefully watched my steps whenever playing in the woods. My brother and I, however, visited the area secretly as now our interest was piqued. When I noticed shiny multi-colored rings on the surface, I reported this to Mom. She concluded that there was an oil well on our property. It became a good diversion; she was now preoccupied with a new situation instead of her failing marriage and legal status.

Visits to her lawyer changed from immigration issues to requesting an analysis be made. In a letter to a geologist in Titusville PA, her lawyer wrote:

Dear Sir,

I have a client who is convinced that she has discovered oil on her property. In my conversations with her I told her that in the event that there was oil on her property that you, by reason of your experience in this kind of matter, would undoubtedly be able to tell her whether or not her discovery is actually oil or not.

The location of the property is such as to be quite provocative. Would you care to run down and take a look at the property to ascertain as to whether it might be of interest to you? Please let me know.

Sincerely yours,

The response from the geologist was: *If the pitch on the northwestern flank of the mountain anticline would not be too severe it might just be possible that this property on the northern flank would be in such a position that there might be oil or gas beneath the surface.* Now we were off to the races. Topics, however, again turned to conflicts in the home. Her attention did not stay long on anything beyond her problems.

Besides having ideas about oil on her property, she was convinced that the property in Germany, which now lay in ruins from the war, had uranium underground. Some local radon inhalation caves were still used for spa treatment. Radon is a naturally occurring radioactive gas and comes from the natural breakdown of uranium. When ingested the brine water contains radon, which was thought to be a cure for arthritis, heart ailments, and general weakness. Letters ensued to German authorities.

We were not regular church attenders. My mother had refused to belong to any formal organization after the horrors of the Nazi regime. We were raised with a modern scientific understanding of the world and the universe. My mother and her brother had grown up in Germany with a God-fearing Nanny. She was hired to care for my sickly uncle, and remained with the family until they were grown. Her influence was gentle and kind, but the children were not allowed to practice piano, work in the garden, or even do needlepoint on Sundays. It was to be a day of rest and reverence to the Almighty.

To Mom, God was a Supreme Being, not a man in the sky, and Jesus was a wise and caring prophet, not the only Son of God. How could her oppressed Jewish friends be condemned to hell if their tradition did not recognize Jesus as the Messiah, who himself was a Jew? Why should innocent people suffer? Our family recited a German prayer before meals, and religious holidays were observed. In addition, reverence for life, as taught by Albert Schweitzer, the noted humanitarian, was highly esteemed. In this and other ways, Mom sought order and meaning.

The local Lutheran church In Germany bordered the property of their hotel. Eventually my mother became aggravated that the church was becoming a business with the properties they managed. At the time, citizens were required to pay taxes to the state church, whether they believed its teachings or not. My mother had serious disagreements with the church as she protested the mistreatment of the Jews. She watched in dismay as her own country, renowned for its churches and universities, ignored a tide of extreme nationalism.

Her distress climaxed when the local parish purchased her mother's bombed-out property for almost nothing. The rubble of the hotel was cleared, and an apartment building was built, with rent collected by the church. The stipulation was that my grandmother be given housing, at no cost, for the remainder of her life. However, instead of an apartment with bath and shower, she was given two rooms with only a hot plate and a bathroom without a shower. Nevertheless, there was a balcony with a view of the majestic rock towering out of the river.

My grandmother didn't complain, and saved the money that the government issued to homeowners of bombed properties. In her older years she became legally blind, and received compensation for this also. What no one suspected was that she would live to ninety-eight years of age! Upon her death these funds were helpful to Mom in her retirement.

At home on Sunday mornings my mother, brother and I gathered around the grand piano and had our own church service. One of her favorite pieces that she played while we sang was "Don't Forget to Pray":

Ere you left your room this morning,
Did you think to pray?
Oh, how praying rests the weary! Prayer will change the night to day;
So, when life seems dark and dreary, don't forget to pray.

When you met with great temptations, did you think to pray?
When your heart was filled with anger, did you think to pray?

Did you plead for grace, my brother?
That you might forgive another who had crossed your way?

The second verse showed her intentions, not only for others, but also for herself. These were difficult for her to accomplish. She regularly used scripture verses to influence us. Two of her favorites were "You cannot serve two masters" and "A house divided cannot stand." They were to ensure complete devotion to her.

Another song on her "play list" was "Wonderful Word of Life:"

Sing them over again to me,
Wonderful words of life;
Let me more of their beauty see,
Wonderful words of life.

Words of life and beauty
Teach me faith and duty;
Beautiful words, wonderful words,
Wonderful words of life.

The words of the song were again hard for her to live up to, though she desired it. I knew in my heart she didn't want to be the person she had become. I saw the good in her, and loved her for that. Besides, she taught me many powerful life lessons. I admit some of the annoying lessons have remained with me to this day. Frugality was a huge issue. She had been through two world wars, and wastefulness was a sin. I could never turn on a light if I could find something in the dark. In setting the table we were instructed to only use the silverware needed for that meal, which was to save water.

On calm days, we took trips to cultural events and historic places, now without my father. These included Hyde Park, Philadelphia, Jamestown, Williamsburg, Washington, and New York City. I was the bright and cheery sibling, my brother the quiet and sullen one. He resented my positive attitude, and at times kicked me under the table to see if I'd get mad. During summer vacation the three of us vacationed at Asbury Park on the New Jersey shore.

In the late 1990's, while selling the old house for funds for our mother's nursing care, I found letters where my father and mother tried in vain to understand each other. My mother's delusions kept her from seeing my father's point of view, no matter how hard he tried. I read these letters with immense sadness:

In the past you asked me to give you explanations in writing. I did this even when it appeared to be nonsense. Today I write the following comments, and do it with all seriousness in lieu of an oath. I am ready to repeat this before anyone.

During our marriage I have never told you a conscious lie. This in itself should be sufficient.

During this time no other women came close to me besides shaking hands.

I have never consciously done anything to make you suspicious or to encourage you to draw wrong conclusions. Quite the opposite, it is my great misfortune in life, that you married me without confidence in me. This created a new distrust and became a vicious circle.

I never said anything unfavorable or complained about you to others.

The children never heard a bad word about you from me. I always encourage our son to tell the truth.

I never played tricks like hiding the silverware nor have I deliberately destroyed anything of yours. I have never looked into your papers, opened your pocketbook, held any letters back or never read them.

I never did anything on purpose to delay your immigration affairs. Quite the opposite, I tried to speed up the process whenever in my power.

I have loved you more than I have loved anyone else. Your mistrust and my inability to quell it have ruined our happiness. More important than you or me are the children, to whom we have the obligation to have a harmonic home.

Your Husband

A year later, and only two months before she left him, my mother replied:

I have given you a long time, because I wanted to believe in you and your otherwise good sides. The contents of your letter last year did not prove that.

A long time ago I answered your letter verbally, that your request for reconciliation, as bitter as it is, and I could never accept it. I would automatically agree to be guilty.

But you, remembering your otherwise good sides, you should have been able to not only learn to overcome, but also keep away from such methods of creating destructive confusion, which can never be thought of as a joke.

I had asked you often enough, as the children did too, to leave us alone for a while. Even here you completely ignored my plea which would have been best for all of us. To know that the house was entered, or perhaps you yourself entered it but denied it to me.

It is not alone for my sake necessary to make a change, which includes any interference from your side for a while, but it is the responsibility and duty toward the children especially for our son who is in the most dangerous period of puberty. He recently indicated "When I am alone with you and my sister, and some mischief happens, I at least know that I have done it."

Certain occurrences in our first home in Munich and then again in Frankfurt happened, for which I should never be to blame. This gives me an understanding that it was repeated here too.

Your Wife

My father was in Germany for four weeks on business in 1955. As he was returning to America, we secretly left for Germany. It was our first time there since arriving in the United States. When my father opened the door to our house, it was empty and we were gone.

In Germany my grandmother greeted us with reserve as she was aware of my mother's problems. She had become an ally of our father. With a childhood friend of my mother's they'd arranged for her to be admitted to a sanitarium. At the last moment, however, the friend revealed their plans, and she refused to go. How differently things might have been if she had consented.

After months of not knowing for sure where we were, my father made a return trip to Germany. There he told our mother he would reconcile if she acknowledged her imaginings were not real. She denied having any problems, and he filed for divorce. A certified letter, containing a review of some occurrences, from my father's business partner to the courts followed:

Soon after the family moved to State College, she came without the knowledge of her husband to complain about him in the presence of her eleven-year-old son. We did our best to convince her that her accusations were nonsense. She also went to common friends and appeared there in a similar manner.

I was together with him on a daily basis. He never complained about difficulties in his marriage until I asked him, and then he blamed it on his wife's nerves, which caused her to see everything in an exaggerated light.

Some of the absurd accusations were that he had hidden silverware in the attic to cause his wife to blame others for stealing it. In another situation, he was supposed to have arranged a receptacle for a record player in such a way that when she would have attempted to use it, she would have gotten possibly a fatal shock. Once again, the eleven-year-old son was called as a witness. All attempts on my part to show her that handling the defective plug would have been harmless went unrealized by her.

When she left with the two children without any note to her husband, he, after four months of not knowing where his family was set out to

Germany. When he returned, he told me that she refused any discussion, and that because of this he proceeded with filing for divorce.

It would be eleven months before my mother, brother, and I returned to America. During this time my father corresponded with my brother. One of these letters revealed the pain of the separation:

Happy Birthday to you! I hope that you all will have a wonderful time in Germany. I do not even know where you are. Mother did not tell you and you, of course, did not know that my birthday was on the 15th of June. I had at least for that day expected to hear from you all.

I have sent your grandmother money for your birthday. Buy yourself a present and for mother some flowers. I am very lonesome here in the house, and am missing you and your sister very much. I just came back from Atlantic City where I was for a convention and got a terrible sunburn on the last day when we spent three hours on the beach.

Next week I have to go to Detroit for two days and shall be back home on your birthday. Say hello to Lottie Barbara, and tell her to draw a little picture for me to send on her birthday July 12.

Please see to it that mother goes to a doctor and does something for her health.

With love to all of you, and to you especially on your birthday.
Father

By now my mother and grandmother were arguing constantly, and once again I sought a place to escape. Mom rented a small apartment and we were periodically enrolled in the local school. The standards of the school were so high that I was placed in second grade instead of third. School supplies included a fountain pen but no pencils, workbooks but no tablet paper, chalkboard for practicing writing and math, all in a leather backpack.

We were taught multiplication tables in math through number 10. Printing was not allowed, only cursive writing. There was no recess with swings and slides. Once I was paddled for tearing a page out of a work-book. If a mistake was made, you had to write an X over it and do it again. I was not used to such strict rules but learned to comply. My brother had similar experiences, but was not held back. He even excelled under the rigors of their educational system, and was in the academic track for science, just like his father.

The winter was particularly cold that year. Visiting friends in Braubach we discovered the Rhine River had turned to solid chunks of ice at various locations. It was so frozen that we could climb over the ice to the other side. This was only the fourth time in modern history that it happened.

Spring finally arrived, and I spent hours playing with girlfriends along the banks of the Nahe River. I was blithely unaware how difficult life would become upon our return to America. With the divorce final, my brother and I were told never to see our father again. We set sail on a Holland America ship that spring, and as we entered our house, we found it empty of all my father's belongings. On the dining room table, sat the little pretzel man, this time holding a note that just said "I'm sorry, children." Hiding my tears, I ran upstairs to my room.

With all their problems my father had avoided our mother so much that I have few memories of him. After teaching classes at the university, he went straight to his consulting office. There he and his partner were now working with a German firm on a new diesel engine that ran quieter and used less fuel than other engines. They hoped an American company would be interested in their patent.

Court proceedings began for parental custody and visitation rights. In those days custody was almost always granted to the mother. I was ten years of age when the dreaded questioning by the judge in closed chambers occurred. I felt sick hearing my brother lie about our home during the interview. I blindly did the same. Our mother had drilled us what to say, including that our father was a terrible person.

The Court of Common Pleas gave their summary requiring equal visitation rights:

And now, after hearing the petition in the above matter, and since it appears to the Court that the differences between the parents of these children are insurmountable, and it further appears that the petitioner has been supporting the children and is ready to pay the college or university expenses of the son, it is therefore, ordered that the father shall, beginning Sunday, and every other Sunday thereafter, from 2:00 until 6:30 PM have custody of the two children until such time as the son enters college or university; thereafter he shall have association with the daughter every other Sunday during said hours. In the event such custody becomes impossible or unpleasant, a further order will be considered in an effort to make a satisfactory adjustment.

What would normally have been a happy time at Christmas in our father's new apartment, was instead lonely and forlorn. His tree was tiny in the small living room. The little angel that was on the top of the tree still sits on my bookcase.

Another court hearing was held the following year. The order concluded:

It is further recommended that the parents of these two children refrain from any effort to influence the said children against either parent, and give the children every opportunity to arrive at their own conclusions concerning their parents, without pressure or force on the part of either parent.

The orders were never followed. I was beginning to see the toll this was taking on my brother, who idolized his father. After each visit he was subjected to questioning and accusations. His stuttering grew worse. Trying to escape, he climbed out the second story window of our house onto the porch. When my mother discovered he was missing she turned on me, screaming until I confessed that he had run away. I saw my father only three times, though the memories of these outings remain clear.

8. ATTEMPTING NORMAL

In lucid moments, Mom attempted to do normal things. State College didn't have a department store, so we drove fifty miles to Gables in Altoona. Before the divorce we shopped in the upstairs department; after the divorce we shopped in the bargain basement. On the way home, we stopped at our favorite restaurant, requesting the same waitress. Upon learning the waitress was a seamstress, my mother asked her to make a doll wardrobe as a birthday surprise.

The wardrobe had more than just dresses. It included a skater's outfit with skates, ballerina outfit with shoes, wedding dress and veil, and a nightgown with housecoat and slippers. The seamstress was a mature woman with heavy makeup. To my disappointment she painted rouge circles on Sandy's cheeks, making my doll look unnatural. There was something strange about red rouge on my dolls. These many outfits are now enjoyed by our grand-daughters.

That summer we drove to Philadelphia to see the Liberty Bell and tour Independence Hall. Though I was only twelve, I wanted a copy of the Declaration of Independence for my birthday. Mom secretly bought it, and surprised me in a unique way. In the first box was another, then another, and another until I came upon the rolled copy. I was perhaps drawn to the Declaration of Independence for various reasons.

The stress of separation and divorce was so debilitating for my father that his health suffered. Following a diagnosis at the Mayo Clinic in Rochester, MN, the doctors recommended he remarry. My father returned to Germany, this time to marry his former high school sweetheart, who was widowed. During the World War II both she and her lawyer husband were captured and held in a Russian work camp. In the senseless strain of being commanded to break rocks, her husband lost his mind and died. She was freed only because she could teach braille piano music to a blind child of a high-ranking Russian officer.

When my father returned to America with his new wife, he tried again to gain visitation rights, and court proceedings resumed. I watched with dread each time a government car pulled up to our house, the sheriff handing my mother another contempt of court order. Numerous trips to law offices followed, and I went along being too young to stay at home.

I waited for my mother in the receptionist's office, thinking as I watched the secretary type that this must be the most glamorous job in the world. I admired her painted nails, red lipstick, and perfectly styled hair. To keep myself occupied, I brought along my little red suitcase containing my German bendable dolls. It was always the same scenario-- father, mother, brother, and sister-- pretending to be a family.

Looking for hopeful things, a favorite movie was Walt Disney's "Pinocchio," and I loved the song Jiminy Cricket sang:

When you wish upon a star
Makes no difference who you are,
Anything your heart desires
Will come to you.
If your heart is in your dream
No request is too extreme,
When you wish upon a star
Like dreamers do.

I felt that I too could have my dreams come true. At the same time, I knew my brother and I were lying to protect ourselves. The tale of Pinocchio's nose getting longer each time he told a lie added to my anxiety. As evening shadows fell, my mother's irritations worsened. She collected legal books busily underling laws she thought applied to her. Hurtful accusations by her toward my brother persisted, as he continued to see my father. Even though he suffered this abuse, he managed to hide his pain by getting straight A's.

My brother was popular in a shy way with a dry sense of humor and sharp wit. He seldom, however, invited friends to our house, for fear they would detect something wrong. In his senior year, he was chosen most intelligent in his class, and given a monetary award from a local research company. Fellow students thought he was brilliant but troubled. At the time I had an awful premonition he wouldn't be able to succeed in life. The relentless accusations had done their damage, and what I feared eventually became true.

Discovering his high school yearbook, I wept while reading the acknowledgments under his photo that showed such promise. *Scientifically minded, spends spare time with a slide rule or science book, enjoys classical music, and doesn't object to being teased.* This last comment stung, because I knew that teasing hurt his feelings. He was embarrassed about his buck teeth, and his slight German accent.

Despite her behavior at home, Mom was paradoxically generous to those outside the family. She volunteered to collect funds for the local Red Cross. To achieve a larger donation, she designed and colored cut-out paper rabbits for Easter decorations. The more paper rabbits bought, the bigger the contribution. Donations soared, and she became the top fundraiser in the county.

Mom had a socially conscious side that I admired. The plight of Native Americans greatly disturbed her. Twice a year she'd send a small check to both St. Labre Indian School in Montana and St. Joseph Indian School in South Dakota. She also supported two paralyzed veterans' groups as well Boys Town in Nebraska. I continued to contribute to these same charitable organizations.

During the Christmas season, fraternity houses at Penn State did community service. Between Mom and the fraternity, several car loads of poor children from our valley were taken to a Christmas party at one of the expansive fraternity houses, complete with an enormous Christmas tree and visit from Santa. I stood in my new department store dress feeling out of place, but smiled and helped hand out gifts.

Some winters were less harsh than others, and the roads wider. Getting stuck in the snow was less frequent. My brother and I went ice skating at the home of a neighbor, whose name happened to be Robert Frost. I had heard Mom read and quote poems by Frost such as "The Road Not Taken," and I thought this might be the famous poet. They were a gracious couple allowing us to use their woodland pond, which seemed magical to me, framed by tall evergreen trees that cast long shadows on the ice. Some days the lady of the house brought hot chocolate, or lit a fire in the outdoor pit so we could warm our hands. When the elderly couple passed away, a sign went up, "No Trespassing," and we never went back.

Among Mom's other positive qualities was a love of poetry. Yet I had a hard time understanding how she could be so sentimental at some times and so cruel at others. A familiar poem hung on our wall was "Take Time":

Take time to think, thoughts are the source of power.
Take time to play, play is the secret of perpetual youth.
Take time to read, reading is the fountain of wisdom.
Take time to pray, prayer can be a rock of strength in time of trouble.
Take time to love, loving is what makes living worthwhile.
Take time to be friendly, friendships give life a delicious flavor.
Take time to laugh, laughter is the music of the soul.
Take time to give, any day of the year is too short for selfishness.

On our front door hung a wrought iron plaque with the Golden Rule: *Do unto others as you would have them do unto you.* Another favorite phrase was: *Wish me what you will, God will give you ten times more.* I was again bewildered how anyone could have such double standards.

Play was an important part of my day. Since our house was far from neighbors, play dates were arranged. A stream ran through the property, and at one place it divided, spilling over rocks and trees making the area to look like a map of North and South America. My girlfriends and I spent hours in our imaginary countries. From time to time we'd switch countries as we sang and danced around the narrow tree trunks. We even knew songs from the recently released movie "South Pacific" Mom taught us at an early age to accept those who were different. As an immigrant myself I took the words to heart:

> *You've got to be taught*
> *To hate and fear,*
> *You've got to be taught*
> *From year to year,*
> *It's got to be drummed*
> *In your dear little ear,*
> *You've got to be carefully taught.*
> *You've got to be taught to be afraid*
> *of people whose eyes are oddly made,*
> *And people whose skin is a different shade*
> *You've got to be carefully taught.*

We raised rabbits, soon discovering that they multiply rapidly. A wooden cage was built, as well as a wire pen that allowed the rabbits to play on the grass. A willing jack-of-all trades was procured for carpentry projects. The handyman was out of work, lived a few miles away, and was my first experience of witnessing poverty. The family didn't own a car, so we picked him up, often bringing food for their family. He was married, with two handicapped daughters living at home. Their house was in shambles, but kindness was evident in the humble dwelling. At times they greeted us with gifts of homemade relish and jam.

All kinds of needy people lived in our valley, and we made a point of bringing food to them on special occasions. One of these families frequently sent their older children to help us tend the garden, and we'd invite them to stay for lunch. The oldest boy, noticing the chopped parsley on his omelet, to our amusement, remarked that he and his sister didn't eat grass.

In the late 1950's, Civil Defense signs, a yellow circle with black triangle, were posted in department stores and public buildings, pointing the way to the nearest fall-out shelters. In school we practiced "duck and cover" drills, in a vain attempt to protect ourselves in case of a nuclear attack. I was hoping the world would last at least until Christmas, then until my next birthday. This was another source of anxiety for me to cope with.

Soon I realized with melancholy that my childhood was slipping away, and I could not stop it. I loved playing with my dolls, and pretend cooking in my tiny play kitchen, but I knew I had to grow up. It was an upsetting realization. Even today I get a lump in my throat when I hear the song "Toyland":

> Toyland, toy land
> little girl and boy land,
> While you dwell within it
> You are ever happy there.
> Childhood's joy land
> Mystic merry toy land,
> Once you pass its borders
> You can never return again.

The school bus stop was a mile from our house, on an isolated road with no other homes except a hunting cabin and a trailer. While my brother was in school, we'd walk together in the morning and afternoon. During the forty-five-minute bus ride, my friend and I passed the time singing, often to the dismay of the other students. She had an amazing voice, and I sometimes thought she could have become a country star. Instead she had a baby out of wedlock, and never left the valley.

I was in sixth grade when my brother graduated from high school. After that Mom didn't allow me to walk alone. On our dirt road lived a single man who happened to be an exhibitionist. Everyone knew of his problem. He was driven every day to work on the township road crew. He was a pitiful, lonely man in his small trailer. Few cars traveled this road and he was never reported. His life ended in a truck accident when I was in tenth grade.

Our closest neighbors were a man and wife with grown children and an unfriendly dog named "Hey Boy." One by one, the mother and father of our dogs arrived as strays. They'd bark at Hey Boy, and sometimes wouldn't let the neighbor out of her garage. Soon a fence around our courtyard was built, and we like Tom Sawyer white-washed the boards.

One morning I looked out of my bedroom window to see my beloved cat "Mousie" lying motionless on the lawn. My worst fears were realized-- Hey Boy had killed her. Now this little companion was gone. Over the years I'd bid farewell to more little friends, and soon a pet cemetery was located at the edge of the property. We had few passing cars on our back road, but lots of horseback riders. Our valley even had its own rodeo on a horse farm back in the woods. It was a welcomed diversion that we could walk to, sit on the wooden bleachers, and watch cowboys ride untamed horses.

When my mother's car was not at the bus stop, I was to get off at a neighbor's home. It was there I learned to eat different foods, such as milk bread and raw potatoes with salt. Not having a TV in our home, it was a treat to watch Popeye the Sailor Man, American Bandstand, and later The Edge of Night. Their oldest daughter and I spent hours and playing make-believe and dress-up. When I was seventeen, she and her mother were killed in a car accident on a major highway.

Despite our meager circumstances, books and culture were valued in our home. We were one of the few families that had built-in bookshelves, filled with both German and American classics. In calm moments, Mom played classical music on the grand piano. When I heard her play Mozart or Chopin, I knew her world was okay, and breathed easier. Not able to afford concert tickets, we attended free music recitals at the university. On the way home we'd stop at the Dutch Pantry restaurant ordering the only thing we could afford, a cup of soup and salad. I always asked "Could we please have rolls and butter instead of crackers." This was calculated because they were more filling. Eventually the waitresses recognized us and added extra rolls to the basket, which we wrapped in a napkin and took home.

We received household monies sent by my father. Much of this was spent on trips to law and immigration offices in Philadelphia, Washington, and New York City, as well as local lawyers. If we didn't have money for these, we took our slide projector, accordion, or violin to a pawn shop. Out of embarrassment we frequented a shop that was located twenty miles away.

It was hoped I had my mother's musical abilities, so I took piano lessons. My teacher was a college freshman who charged less than others. Between his inexperience and my mother's criticism, lessons became unbearable. In addition, the car broke down or she got sick, and eventually lessons ended. When I was old enough, I joined a local 4-H Club. The 4-H pledge sounded perfect to me as I memorized and repeated it at meetings. The concept of Head, Heart, Hands, and Health became my philosophy of life.

I pledge my head to clearer thinking,
My heart to greater loyalty,
My hands to larger service,
and my health to better living,
for my club, my community, my country, and my world.

The skills of 4-H, including cooking and sewing, served me well in youth and later life. Although like the piano, dance, riding lessons, and Brownies, 4-H Club was also discontinued. I learned never to get my hopes too high. I became familiar with cooking at home, preparing a few of the specialties beloved in my grandmother's hotel in Germany. Meals were basic, except for a scrumptious dessert called soufflé a la comfiture. It was a fluffy baking soda omelet folded with jelly in the center, and a dusting of confectioners' sugar on top. In our coal burning heatrola, an iron poker was heated and laid on top of the sugar to caramelize it. The smell was heavenly.

The pattern of taking me out of school continued, and my grades slipped. My mother was still worried about her negative status on her immigration card. Visits to officials now included congressmen who couldn't supply answers. With her obsession about her legal status, and now the divorce, she was lost in a fog of illusions. Even an appointment at the Pentagon in Washington didn't yield any results. Upon leaving, the General simply said, "Ma'am, just go home and be a good woman."

9. ONE DAY AT A TIME

Though we didn't have much money, to my astonishment Mom never totally despaired. She believed that the universe would provide for us, and surprisingly she was often right. Living far from the main highway we rarely had visitors, but one afternoon a World Book Encyclopedia salesman knocked at our door. He had been referred by an acquaintance, and was a kindly gentleman who promised that my grades would improve if we purchased his twenty-volume set of encyclopedias. She agreed to the $10.00 monthly payment plan, and proudly displayed the set on our bookshelf. Though it was a great product, it did not automatically raise my grades.

Several weeks later a letter arrived, signed by the president of Field Enterprises, inviting her to become a representative. What she didn't realize was that it was a form letter sent to every customer. She quickly accepted. Now instead of sitting in law offices, I waited in the car during her sales calls. On one call, as it was getting dark, the man of the house came out and said "You're too pretty to sit outside alone." I had never really heard the word pretty said about me.

Soon commissions were coming in, and we had extra money. Instead of buying clothes from clearance racks, I now occasionally picked out full priced ones. Mom was a good salesperson, and her persistence wore down the customers until they purchased. She also used guilt, insinuating that parents certainly wanted the best for their children. In addition, she coined the phrase "Just do it!" long before it became a famous slogan. Her confidence rose with each order. When customers expressed embarrassment over a messy house, she'd reply, "It is better to have dust on the furniture than dust on the soul of a child." I practically choked each time I heard it.

One of her early prizes was an automatic washing machine to replace the old electric wringer washing machine. Wringer washers were problematic in that each piece of clothing had to be fed through two tight rollers that squeezed the water out as the clothes dropped into another wash tub. The process was done again so the rinse cycle could be completed. It was an arduous process in the cold damp cellar. My fingers sometimes got caught between the rollers if I wasn't careful. Then there were the times that my brother and or I forgot to finish the laundry, and it sat in the rinse water for days. When this happened, the clothes gave an awful odor. In an attempt to prove that she thought someone was breaking into our house and spraying our clothes with chemicals, she took the smelly laundry to a professor's home, and dumped it on their table. In repulsion they brushed the clothes away. I watched in embarrassment.

It was apparent, at times, Mom wanted to make me happy. For my tenth birthday she asked what my wish was, and I replied to wake-up watching TV. She was proud to say she didn't believe in having a TV in the home. However, I felt left out when friends talked about waking up on Saturday mornings to see kid shows and cartoons. To grant my wish, we drove over Skytop Mountain to a motel on Rt. 220. I was overjoyed until check-out time.

To celebrate our new financial success, I was given a choice for my twelfth birthday of either a pony or a pond. I opted for the pond which also increased the value the property. Besides my brother and I had taken riding lessons earlier in the year, and I found myself anxious around these powerful creatures. My imaginary North and South America play area ended when the stream water was needed to be channeled into the pond. A wooden dock in the center of the pond was a welcomed treat. On Sunday afternoons I'd sit reading the "Grit," a weekly newspaper popular in rural America. Noon was a good time to get a tan, or red burn, without knowing the dangers of using baby oil as sun tan lotion. It was a time to rest from labors.

With her new job earning we bought our first car. It was a lemon. The supposedly new car had actually been in an accident and was reconditioned. After years of repairs and bills, it became another example of that favorite word, vandalism. The doomed car finally died.

It was winter and I had a bad ear ache along with a fever. We couldn't get to a doctor because of darkness and icy roads. My mother's standard remedy for most illnesses was a hot bath, hot water bottle, and blankets piled high. She'd sit beside us wiping the sweat from our face. This time, instead of forcing out the fever, it pushed liquid through my eardrum and I developed tinnitus.

Power was out again for a week after another major snow storm. After my brother left for college, I was the one to carry coal buckets from the cellar, and empty the ashes from the stove. The ashes were then scattered on the icy road, or shoveled in a pile for the next storm. The coal buckets were so heavy I worried my arms and legs would look like a man's. This was about the time I sought preteen guidance from the 1958 popular book "Twixt Twelve and Twenty" by Pat Boone.

Riding the school bus home, I watched with sympathy as a pretty girl from a poor family, exactly the same age as myself got off the bus. Her shoulders were hunched, and her expression was always bleak from the burden of work of being the first of seven children. I was afraid I would soon look like her.

Sometimes we didn't have enough coal to get through the day, saving it for warmth overnight. Since the woods had been lumbered twenty years before, the trunks of trees broke easily with an ax. There was also the danger of a flu fire if the soot from the stove pipes to the chimney weren't cleaned twice a year. When I finished scraping the black soot from the pipes, soot covered my face framing my blue eyes. Looking in the mirror I appeared like Cinderella, and feared I was like her, yet too young to have a Prince Charming.

My brother, meanwhile, had few friends who understood or appreciated him. However, another gifted and talented student often sat beside him during the long bus rides. He and my brother discussed among other things inventing noise cancelling headphones way back then. The idea was not pursued, yet if it had been it would have been successful. The friend later earned a doctorate in mathematics, went on to teach, and became a chairman of the board at a college.

My brother's activities in school included marching band, basketball team, and social dances. When I was in high school, there was too much confusion at home for me to participate in extracurricular activities. In his senior year my brother was chosen as a graduation speaker. In the back of the auditorium, my father and his new wife were seated, but we were not to talk to them.

Applications and college visits began, and we took my brother for interviews at Princeton, Cornell, Duke, and University of Virginia. He was accepted at all of these, and chose UVA. However, deadlines were missed, and he had to start the first semester by correspondence at Penn State where our father was a professor. The winter term was about to begin, and he planned to drive to drive to UVA in our father's Studebaker. Mother refused to let him to go, and called the sheriff.

Though the hour was late, the sheriff knew where we lived since he had been there many times. My sixth-grade girlfriend was visiting for the evening, and we were preparing hamburgers. We watched nervously as the hamburgers shriveled and burned in the frying pan, by this time no one was hungry, and the meat was thrown out.

I was embarrassed in front of my friend, especially as the yelling grew louder. My brother called his friend's parents, but to no avail, and it was now almost midnight. When the sheriff arrived, he managed to calm everyone down, and my brother drove to our father's home, not to UVA.

Now another deadline was missed. He continued at PSU and moved into a dormitory. A huge rift had occurred; we hardly saw my brother after that.

Life got stranger. Every time we left the house three locks were used, including padlocks, to secure the door. Mother thought someone was entering the house, but never said who, and by now I didn't question it. If I said something, I became the object of further accusations, so I didn't. When the locks weren't enough security, a thread was strung across the door to prove an intrusion. I prayed the wind or a woodland creature would not break the string. Sometimes it remained intact, other times not. Fearing we were being watched, she made me lean down on the front seat of the car so people would think I was home as we drove out of the valley. She convinced herself that people were breaking into the house to disturb her important papers or do vandalism.

Her suspicions now turned toward me. She'd complain of stomach pains, and suspected I was making her sick. I dreaded when milk had been left on the counter by her the night before, soured, and curdled in her coffee. Perplexed that she thought I was poisoning her, I'd escape into the woods.

My brother and I were mystified and pained as we watched our mother's paranoia increase. He was given a chemistry set by our father, and soon afterward several bottles of chemicals were missing. She had removed ones that could possibly have poisoned her. That Easter, a large ham was purchased that included the customary FDA purple inspection stamp. In her mind the blueish purple dye was evidence that poison had been applied, namely bluestone that was kept in the house to control the algae in our pond. The ham was thrown out, and replaced with hot dogs. It would have been funny, if it wasn't so tragic. She had told us of the persecutions during Nazi times, causing us to wonder if her unexplainable distrust might have also stemmed from the horrors of the past.

The local grocer in Potters Mills and his family lived not far away. They were kindly people, and their children were about the age as my brother and me. Sometimes they'd invite us to their apartment above the store, and I wondered what they must have thought when my mother told of her fears. Afraid that someone might be listening on her phone calls at home, she made important calls from their phone. In their store she didn't buy instant coffee in large quantities, only small jars, in case someone was poisoning her. At times she made me drink first, I guess as a trial run.

With my brother gone, Mom was afraid to spend nights alone in the house, so each evening we packed and drove across the valley to the home of an elderly couple. Their upstairs bedroom didn't have heat, so hand-made quilts were piled up to keep us warm. At sunrise we returned home for breakfast, and I got ready for school in a cold house.

Our dogs--Blackie, Brownie, and Rolfie, and Mutsche, their pups, eagerly awaited us when we returned. Even our dogs were dysfunctional. The father and son fought each other, and could be separated only by spray-ing them with water from a hose. Great care and time were consumed in keeping them apart. Before my brother left home permanently, he shoved me into a corner saying "Just wait, you'll be next." He wasn't too far off in his prediction of her behavior toward me. Yet, this was almost mild consid-ering what he had experienced.

My brother studied hard his first semester in college, and received all A's. That summer he worked in one of the labs of the university, and never came home. I missed him, though he was six years older, and some-times teased me for being childish. In his second year of college he joined a fraternity. Not having had a normal social life, he wasn't well equipped to handle freedom, plus his buck teeth was an embarrassment. The process of straightening his teeth only began in his sophomore year. By this time, he was suffering from bouts of depression, to feel better he turned to beer, then marijuana.

By his junior year he had a serious breakdown, and dropped out of college for a semester. Since depression was stigmatized in those days, our father sought treatment for him at a hospital in another town. This was also to prevent his mother from visiting him. Electric shock treatments, common in those days, were administered in the hopes he'd forget his painful memories.

At the hospital my brother revealed to the doctors for the first time what had happened to him. He told the psychiatrists the confessional letters our mother forced him to write were written to promote her and blame our father. He told the doctors that none of the statements were true, that he wrote them only to appease her.

It took me almost thirty years to apologize to my brother for the suffering he endured. I was by then married with children, on a trip to Florida, when I saw him. He was hospitalized after a bad reaction to alcohol. It was a visit I'll never forget. With tears streaming down my face I acknowledged that I knew all along he was innocent. When we returned to the motel, I ran to the bathroom and threw up.

My excuse for not defending my brother in front of my mother had been fear of her retaliation. I had seen what happened to him, and to protect myself refused phone calls, visits, gifts, and money from our father. It was a tough bargain. I was alone, with no one to turn to, no family or friends to help.

Eventually the pawn shop monies were not enough to cover expenses. In the seventh grade I began selling greeting cards and gift items door to door. Soon I had a file of customers, including my favorite sixth grade teacher. She always ordered, and visits to her home were pure delight. I learned much from her about art and creativity, and she showed me what real caring was. Over time she bought and accumulated a set of twelve delicate dessert plates and cups, telling me that she was leaving them to me in her will. Time passed, and I lost touch with her and her adopted daughter, and I didn't inherit the pretty dishes. This favorite teacher deservedly earned a seat at the head table during our wedding reception.

Many of my customers were miles away. I didn't have transportation with the demise of our car, but a friendly lumberman in his big red truck rolled by our house each day. My mother flagged him down, and asked if he could take us to town. This became a routine several times a week. He'd let me off in the area of my customers, and Mom at a grocery store. Fortunately, none of the customers inquired how I got there. He then picked us up, she with her groceries and me with my suitcase of samples. I had to learn to swallow my pride.

My brother graduated from Penn State, and accepted a position as an assistant physicist at the prestigious Lawrence Livermore Radiation Laboratory in the San Francisco area. He would work under Edward Teller, Hungarian born physicist who immigrated to America in the 1930's, and known as the "father of the Hydrogen bomb." We said goodbye to each other at the bus station, yet I couldn't help wondering how this was going to work out. I took a deep breath and sadly waved farewell.

My father and his new wife had moved back to Germany the previous year. While here in America they had hosted many faculty parties, but the adjustment to this country was difficult for her. Therefore, my father accepted the position as head of the Department of Mechanical Engineering at the University of Munich. I never did get to visit the modern, spacious, new home he purchased for his new wife. Later in high school art class, I drew a picture of a house that looked just like his.

Daily life brought new challenges, and my mother experienced back pains. Some mornings it was too painful for her to get out of bed. I took babysitting jobs; this wasn't easy because the parents had to pick me up and drive me home. Besides her back pains and stomach troubles, she complained of angina. Some nights she called for me to bring hot water and vinegar compresses to relieve the pressure. With trembling knees, I ran up and down the steps, fearing she might die.

Living in the woods was initially intriguing for us children. I loved the mystery of the sun and shadows across the street from our house. It was an area made barren from the foresting of trees, and I thought the dark woods beyond the clearing was where Santa had his workshop. When

Mom recognized this, she made footprints in the snow, assuring me this was indeed his workshop. The next morning, I found a box of animal crackers with a note from Santa reminding me to be good. I was older than most kids when I stopped believing.

I was eight years old when on St. Nickolas Day, the German holiday when St Nick brings his big book, a piece of coal or an orange, a bearded figure in a hooded cape knocked at our door. My mother announced that it was St. Nickolas, and I was astounded. He had treats for me, and asked if I had been a good girl. He then proceeded to make himself comfortable on our couch. I was skeptical, and blurted that it was my brother, to which Mom replied, that he was upstairs taking a bath. To complete the charade, she had water running in the bathtub.

The woods were also an adventure for our dogs. They brought home dead rabbits, squirrels, and opossums. When they had cornered a porcupine, it was an ordeal for my brother and me. I held the dog with a bandana around its eyes while my brother extracted the quills from its nose with a pair of pliers.

I heard the dogs barking again and thought it was another porcupine. This time they had surrounded a tree, where a brown bear clung to a branch. The bear was as frightened as we were, as the dogs and I raced home. Other encounters were less scary, like the time a baby opossum wondered onto our porch, its mother lying dead on the road after a car hit it.

It was winter as we put the baby opossum in a box and proceeded to feed it. Seemingly the only option was to have him spend the winter in our attic. We laid out food, and though he never appeared, the food was always gone. At night he wondered between the attic and the ceiling, making scratching sounds. Whenever I had a girlfriend stay overnight, I feared she wouldn't want to come again. Later she told me the experiences at our house were cool. By spring we knew that Peter, his given name, would have to leave.

Our chestnut tree was being pruned, and we asked the workers to arrange the branches so they'd reach the attic window. I opened the window and watched from a distance as Peter made his way down and into the woods, never looking back. Of course, the attic had to be cleaned and aired out. Peter's stay had not been such a great idea.

One of the benefits of my mother's sales job was that some of her customers became our friends. The long and frequent visits she made until they finally bought gave everyone a chance to know each other. Sometimes this was not the case, as when she was greeted at the door with a stern look and the demand that she not come back.

One couple were grandparents of two young boys, in kindergarten and third grade. The boys' parents had been killed three years earlier in a head-on car crash. The older boy suffered severe injuries, including a missing jaw. They were loving people, and when they learned we were alone at Thanksgiving and Christmas, invited us to join them. I learned a lot about kindness from such experiences. Mom later gave the boys piano lessons at their home, and afterwards they'd served us a delicious meal with home-made pie.

On another sales call, a Baptist minister and his family became our friends. My mother was never shy about her religious views, or lack thereof, but they didn't disparage her and were always welcoming. We occasionally attended their church, and on leaving she'd voice comments about the message. The friendship nevertheless endured, and the minister was named her power of attorney after her stroke. I was dismayed that she didn't trust me to be her POA.

In my late teens we called on a school teacher and his family. They too became a source of support. Both sensed something was very different about my mother, but they did not reject her. They were reasonable people who didn't succumb to her endless requests, and he became executor of her will. He also helped me deal with my brother's depressive episodes.

We invited another customer, with a family of ten children, to our home for a German meal. He discovered that our kitchen was a tiny galley kitchen, next to a sunny room remodeled years before while my father was still with us. My mother showed him an advertisement in House Beautiful magazine for Armstrong linoleum featuring a beautiful kitchen. The yellowed advertisement showed a kitchen with gleaming white cupboards and Pennsylvania Dutch designs. The new friend offered to help make this dream come true, between his missionary trips to Suriname, South America.

Work break conversations centered on topics ranging from the cosmos to being born again, though this didn't end their friendship. After many trips to outlet stores in his old pick-up truck, construction, and the painting of folk-art designs on the benches and cupboards, we had our new kitchen. It was a creative project in which we all exalted.

All seemed perfect, except the pattern of the linoleum was discontinued. Over the years, I'd cut rolls of cheap linoleum, as any Armstrong linoleum was unaffordable. There wasn't any heat in the kitchen until we found a two-burner white enameled wood stove. During the hasty remodeling of this room the flooring of the kitchen hadn't been properly insulated, resulting in the water pipes freezing on cold nights. When this happened, I laid on the dirt crawl space with a hair dryer thawing the pipes. I vowed that when I grew up, there would be order and life would be simpler in my home.

It was Christmas and we couldn't afford a tree. On a snowy evening I was surprised to see a pick-up truck stop outside the house. We rarely had traffic except for hunters going to their lodges to hunt deer or bear. When I saw a man pull a little Christmas tree from the back of his truck, I was overjoyed and watched him dust off the fresh snow before he knocked on the door. It was a gift from one of her sales customers, who owned a tree farm in our valley.

I purchased blue lightbulbs for the little tree that sat on a deep windowsill between our bookshelves. It was a German custom for the holidays to decorate with evergreen branches. But the only evergreens on our property were pine; though the sap from the branches smelled good, its scrawny branches never looked like a Christmas tree. On the piano, candles and little wooden German angels surrounded our stately tall porcelain Madonna. She'd been knocked over many times by the dogs as they jumped onto the piano, and glued back together again.

10. HAPPENINGS

During the summer of 1963, my mother thought she had found a law that implicated my father and the government, and we were headed to the nearest immigration office. Yet, we had no car, and it was too far for the lumber trucker to take us. Therefore, a rental Pontiac was procured. On the way back from the rental office, she parked at a hardware store to buy another lock, and was about to get out of the car when a car came speeding by ripping off her door, and depositing it several feet away. My mother was unhurt, but the other driver was furious, his car being a brand-new Cadillac.

The door landed on the lawn of an elderly couple who came out to see what had happened. They allowed my mother to use their telephone. Upon hearing the story of not having a car, they offered their push-button automatic Plymouth. This was one of those serendipitous moments I had learned to count on. We now had a low mileage car in front of our house.

Mom was used to dealing with hired help at their hotel in Germany. She therefore expected prompt and courteous service from sales clerks. We frequented a Sears store on College Avenue across from the main campus in State College. When a transaction with a particular clerk didn't meet her expectations, Mom requested to speak to their supervisor. I was mortified as a teenager. Yet, at this Sears store she bought my first Beatle's album "Please Please Me" as a Christmas present.

A new furniture store was opening at the Easterly Parkway Plaza in State College, and free drawings were held, with no obligation to buy. We registered for a console TV in the drawing, as she was ever hopeful, but I was doubtful since we had never won anything. A few days later, we got a call we'd won! We already had a small TV, a prize from World Book, though it only got two snowy channels using a rabbit ear antenna, Altoona and Johnston. The beautiful walnut cabinet console TV was sold for much-needed cash.

Friday, November 22, 1963, in Dallas, Texas, President John F. Kennedy was assassinated. I was sitting in Business Class at Penns Valley High School when the announcement was made over the intercom that the president had died. Teachers and students sat stunned and crying. School was cancelled for the next three days. At home it was decided the basement walls needed to be whitewashed. Our little transistor radio sat on the shelf while we listened to the services in Washington. During the singing of Ava Maria, I humbly bowed my head, and cried with millions of mourners across the country and around the world.

At first it seemed the California sunshine was working for my brother. He bought a new red Mustang convertible, had an apartment, and started dating. His department heads at the Livermore Laboratory seemed pleased with his work. This began to deteriorate, however, when he was transferred to nuclear research, which, at least in his mind, conjured thoughts of a nuclear holocaust. He always had strong pacifist leanings, Albert Schweitzer being one of his heroes. It was also the late sixties, and the reaction to the Vietnam War was growing. He had been drafted for the Vietnam, but was rejected due to his flat feet.

During the Summer of Love, my brother sent me subscriptions to underground newspapers, such as the "Berkeley Barb," the first and most influential counterculture newspaper. It covered subjects such as the peace and civil rights movements, and other social changes of the youth culture. It was also known for hoaxes, such as dried banana peels could cause a psychedelic high. The paper printed relevant pieces opposing the War, and was a venue for styles, art, and music. When the paper added sexual advertisements, I grew alarmed. A spin-off paper was tried in New York City, but when women staffers became aware of this issue, they stole page layouts and burned them.

For my birthday that year, I received a "Grateful Dead" and a "Jefferson Airplane" album. My brother was increasingly alone, and his world was collapsing. Pain and depression returned, and he resorted once again to alcohol, now shared with newly acquired acquaintances. Marijuana and LSD were also popular during this time. Under their influence, on a beach, he was arrested and lost his job.

My father paid for to get him out of jail, and fly him to Germany. Alcoholism and drug addiction didn't cease. He attempted work at various scientific companies such as Siemens, but wound up being dismissed each time. The friends he associated with there were again on the fringe of society, unhappy with the status quo. Some of them had gone underground, or left for other countries in response to the Vietnam War.

To earn money his jobs included laying cable for a film crew, far removed from his chosen career. Though he found life in Germany exciting, his manic depression set in again, and my father had him institutionalized in a state facility. It was commonly known that anyone who went there didn't come out the same. Heavy drugs were administered, nobody questioned, and he was alone.

His collect calls both from California and now Germany were constant at our house. Under the influence of alcohol his hostilities toward my mother and her abuse of him came out. He was now literally the verbally abusive one, yelling names he had once been called, a tragic déjà vu. With nowhere to go and nobody to turn to, we feared he might take his life.

My mother's health worsened. I found myself skipping school to care for her, and my grades slipped. Depression as such didn't plague me, yet I suffered under low self-esteem. This was about the time that the movie "Pollyanna" with Hayley Mills was released. I was impressed by how she handled situations with a sunny disposition and I imagined being like her!

During these years I looked forward to Sunday morning church services at the Schwab Auditorium on the Penn State campus that my mom and I attended. It was there that I learned to appreciate well-crafted sermons presented by well-known lecturers and ministers. The nine hundred seat facility was usually filled, and a highlight was when the large choir filed out singing the Seven-Fold Amen. It would send chills down my back.

I began to realize that our family was quite different from others. It wasn't just in language but also in customs, interests and styles. I was embarrassed when my mother picked me up at a friend's house wearing her old French beret. She also wore a fake lamb's wool coat during my entire youth. In the fall there was the German wool suit worn year after year. She prided herself on being a non-conformist. If my friends wore popular pump shoes, I had to wear unpopular black and white saddle shoes. I managed to get around this by bringing my pump shoes to school in a paper bag hidden under my coat.

We had strict table manners, and couldn't leave the table without finishing all our food and asking to be excused. I hated boiled fish, and when no one was looking, I'd hide it in a napkin and stash it in my bedroom drawer. Fearing my mother's reaction of not finishing my food, it unfortunately backfired when the smell got so bad that she noticed it. I was horrified when she claimed that someone had sprayed a chemical to upset her. Again, I was in a quandary, not knowing which was worse, to admit it and be punished or not admit it and be punished.

After cleaning my room, I was distressed when I couldn't find my German bracelet charm. My heart sank because it was a gift from my grandmother, and was engraved with: *Gott Schutze Dich, God Protect You.* Needless to say, when Mom discovered it was missing the coming months were unpleasant. Winter passed, and in spring while I was working in the flower bed, underneath my window, I found the charm in the dirt. I tried to explain it must have fallen out when I shook the shag rug, but that didn't help.

Everyday care was overlooked, dental visits, doctor appointments, and health insurance were ignored. Obsessions consumed her as more law books were acquired. She had convinced herself that the X on her immigration card meant "persona non grata," indicating that we had no sponsor in this country. Also, the term "non compos mentis," not in one's right mind, were repeated many times. She rarely saw a doctor, as I think she feared them. Doing her research, she found it takes only three doctors to be committed to a mental institution. The night she scratched an X on my bedroom door, in anger, with a pair of pliers, the tune to the TV series the Twilight Zone came to my mind. After this episode I realized I needed to keep her behavior secret. If someone found out what would happen to me. With no relatives or close friends, it was scary thought.

At times I found her standing in front of a mirror, talking to herself, as if to a lawyer or immigration officer. By now she thought that people were bugging our house. To counteract this, she turned on the faucet in the bathroom, and insisted I sit and listen. She still thought I was an accomplice with my father and brother, although both of them were no longer around.

I became increasingly nervous, fearing always someone would recognize her illness. I tried to conceal my emotions, but my panic attacks in school got worse. I avoided mirrors, not because I was still afraid of a devil there, but because my eyes looked so pained that I hardly recognized myself. My teeth were showing signs of decay. Unlike my brother who had buck teeth, mine were crooked, and I rarely smiled.

Even the dogs had no boundaries. The doors had deep scratches made by our unrestrained dogs. There was simply no order. Yet at other times I admired my Mom's stamina. Despite all the chaos, she came home after work, and went straight to the kitchen to prepare a meal, still wearing her beret.

While in the tenth grade, I was asked by a senior to go to the Prom. To my disbelief, Mom took me to a fine clothing store in State College for a dress. It was made of red taffeta, with thin straps, and a frilly skirt. I was ecstatic. Mom showed caring moments, and I cherished these despite knowing they wouldn't last.

One stipulation was that I meet the young man at his home. It was a magical evening, and the earrings and necklace she gave me I wore at my wedding years later. I must have looked pretty because the young man kept staring at me. He left for college that summer, and we didn't see each other again. He had called, but I was told not to pick up the phone, or give an excuse why I couldn't see him.

Eleventh grade in high school was especially difficult. While classmates had their yearbook pictures taken, I had to miss school. My mother feared my father would use the picture for a passport and take me out of the country. In the yearbook, where my picture should have been, there was just a blank image. My insecurities deepened that year when a teacher caught me talking, and I was called out to continue reading. I had lost my place, my heart raced, and I felt faint. Students around me snickered and joked. My best friend said she could see me shrinking into myself.

My mother informed me we were departing for Germany just as my senior year was about to start. She wanted to contest the divorce within the statute of limitations, and I was to testify she was a good mother. I dreaded this, because what I was going to say. How much more could I cover up and go against my inner reality. Mom's health deteriorated, and the trip was cancelled. By now I feared everything about school, especially my teachers, who appeared oblivious about me and my home situation.

I could not explain the suffering I was experiencing. Who would have believed me? Where were the counselors who could have helped? I had many unexcused absences, yet where was the truant officer? No one seemed to care. After missing several weeks of school, I made the decision to not return to school. My mother seemed almost pleased. Maybe it was my only choice at the time, to avoid a nervous breakdown. When my father heard I was not going back to school, he sent a letter by way of his lawyer. Knowing my mother would not give me the letter, it was sent certified mail.

In it he pleaded with me to graduate, and promised to pay for my education. His closing remarks in his letter were:

Please think for a moment and let me help you find your way. It is unnatural for you to refuse any contact with your father. I know of many cases where the parents are divorced, but in all cases the children stay in contact with both parents, except you. You are not a little child anymore and are more and more responsible yourself for decisions about your personal life. You should know that I love you as much as I love your brother, and that I always tried to do my best for both of you and want to do so in the future.

He was by then living with his second wife in Munich, Germany. The normal thing would have been to receive support from his colleagues mentioned in the letter. However, normal was something I knew very little about. I knew my father was right, but felt crippled. It was as if my legs and now my spirit had been broken, and I could do nothing to change the situation. My mother didn't help it any by yelling I wouldn't amount to anything. I tried to remain true to myself, unlike my brother, who tried to keep the peace. There wasn't any peace anyway.

What I didn't realize, besides not having a high school diploma, was the shame that followed. I withdrew from classmates, and after a while they stopped calling. They never knew what really happened, and perhaps they felt I had rejected them. Embarrassed, I drove to another county to take the GED exam, the equivalency of a high school diploma, and passed. For years and even today, whenever I hear the processional graduation tune "Pomp and Circumstance" a deep sadness washes over me. I would never experience this milestone.

Ashamed I sought friends from other school districts. A new friend was the daughter of a World Book customer, several years younger than I. They lived near a roller-skating rink where we'd spend hours skating and laughing. She also went sailing with me, and in winter sledding down our hill. During my mother's stay at the hospital I was invited to spend several nights at their home. In the morning watching her mix orange juice from a store-bought frozen container, a melancholy feeling came over me. It was a simple act that rarely happened at our house.

I was getting lonelier, and worried how my life would turn out. She and her parents attended an evangelical church, and invited me to come. The minister gave an altar call, an invitation to those who wanted their life to change. If they accepted the Lord all would be well. I nervously walked forward. I felt I had nothing to lose and hoped this might help. All I could do at the altar was weep. Life was still hard.

A few years later my friend was engaged to be married. She had asked me to be a bridesmaid, and I accepted. This was going to be awesome to be part of a wedding party. When I told my mother, however, she said I couldn't do that because we were going to Germany. It turned out we didn't go anyway, I went to the wedding, but only as an attendee. A second wedding was missed when a return flight was cancelled. For that one I had already sown my dress from material the bridesmaids were given. It almost seemed like weddings were jinxed.

I was the one now that kept the house clean and orderly. We probably had the shiniest polished old refrigerator in the neighborhood! That year the movie "The Unsinkable Molly Brown" with Debbie Reynolds was in theaters. She became a role model for me, and the word unsinkable appealed to me. Still it was an unhappy year.

Nothing was working in the house. Even the clocks showed the wrong time. I was accused of setting them incorrectly, causing her to be late. We had an appointment with a dentist for my decaying teeth. The clock again gave the wrong time, we were late, and I was blamed. On the way to the office, sitting in the front seat, I was slapped as I tucked my head between my knees.

In the dentist's waiting room, with reddened eyes, I sat far from her. Ironically, we waited half an hour to be called. It gave me time to compose myself, and come up with yet another excuse should anyone ask. But no one bothered to inquire if something was wrong or if I had been crying.

It would three years later, with my own money, that I went back to have dental work done.

Despite the suffering, I refused to completely despair. Maybe this was because of a genetic gift from my ancestors, or the influence of great words like those of Goethe, which ironically hung on our living room wall:

Gut verloren, etwas verloren!   *Possessions lost, something is lost;*
Musst rasch dich befinnen   *You must make your move*
Und Neues gewinnen.   *to reacquire them.*
Ehre verloren, viel verloren.   *Honor lost; much is lost;*
Musst Ruhm gewinnen,   *You must win it back,*
Da werden die Leute   *Otherwise people will*
Sich anders befinnen.   *Think poorly of you.*
Mut verloren, alles verloren!   *Courage lost; everything is lost!*

All along I felt I would become stronger, like Nietzsche's quote *What does not kill me makes me stronger*. Though at the time I didn't know this quote, it was just an inward feeling that keep me going.

My father stopped sending our household allowance money, hoping this would change my mind, and I'd return to school. Instead this made things even worse. My babysitting jobs didn't bring much money, and I asked for employment as a waitress at the Penn Hi Boy restaurant. Now after work, I'd stop at a lumber mill, still in my uniform, and loaded chunks of wood into the trunk of the car for our wood burning stove. Cost per trunk load was $2.00.

I discovered, to my surprise, that people actually liked me. Waitressing turned out to be good for me financially and emotionally. Generous tips followed, and customers requested to be seated in my section. I learned much about human nature and how to relate to people. My German heritage, where good manners were emphasized, also helped. As my services were appreciated, my self-esteem improved.

Needing to branch out, I befriended a college student in our valley. We had something in common as she also came from a troubled home.

Her friendship meant a lot to me practically and emotionally. She offered to drive me to my job that year on her way to school. During snowy winter months she'd drive as far as she could before the road became too treacherous, and I'd ski to meet her. She was dedicated person who later became a beloved teacher.

I became the caretaker of our property. Instead of cutting back on flower beds, I expanded them. Building stone walls around flower beds was a particular source of satisfaction. To overcome and cope with what was happening I kept busy. It was then I discovered the pleasure of accomplishing a task. When the perennials grew out of control, I figured I could earn extra money by selling them. Every bit of income helped to pay for our groceries. Raspberry and blueberry bushes grew in the area, and they too were packed and sold. While working I loved to sing:

> *Someday I'll wish upon a star*
> *Wake up where the clouds are far behind me*
> *Where trouble melts like lemon drops*
> *High above the chimney top*
> *That's where you'll find me*
> *Somewhere over the rainbow*
> *Bluebirds fly*
> *And the dreams that you dare to*
> *Oh why, oh why can't I?*

I managed to have some semblance of a social life with university students who dropped in for dinner at the Penn Hi-Boy. I dated a few, allowing myself to fall in love with one young man, who had made the mistake of offering to help with jobs around our house. He ended up planting rows of hemlock trees from the woods, while I brought him iced tea and cake. When my mother became aware that I really like him, I wasn't allowed to take his phone calls, and he stopped coming. In the future, I'd have to have friendships without her knowledge.

Further up on Atherton Street the Autoport a well-known land-mark paid higher wages. Walking in I asked to speak to the owner, and was hired on the spot. Tips were higher as many more Penn State football fans came for dinner after a game. I was happy to work with both experienced waitresses and college students. One older waitress grew jealous when my apron hung low filled with tips, and began calling me "Lotus Blossom." In those days coins as well as dollars were the tips. I was never sure if this was a compliment or an insult.

To my distress, I had become suspect in vandalizing our car, and wasn't allowed a driver's license. While parked at a drive-in restaurant, I attempted to reason with my mother why I'd want to jeopardize my own driving. She made a scene why I hadn't helped to clear her name and rep-utation in the divorce papers. I never again tried to reflect reality; it was obvious she was incapable of hearing it. But it remained embarrassing, with only a learner's permit, to be dropped off and picked up at work.

However, I couldn't get to work because she couldn't drive with her back issues. I would be twenty before insisting on a driver's license. I'd now take her to her piano student homes. While she gave lessons, I'd shop for groceries with the payment given before the lesson. It was there I learned to study supermarket flyers and do coupon shopping. My earnings were for living expenses, hers for endless repairs.

Her back pain was so bad that one night I panicked and called an ambulance. I was still in my teens, and thought she was dying. I ran and brought her brandy. In the ambulance, I poured the brandy in her mouth, and the EMT's didn't stop me. I wonder what the nurses at the hospital thought of her reeking of alcohol. Whenever leaving the house, she made sure to have a McCormick flavoring bottle filled with brandy in case of angina attacks. At twenty-one, I stood timidly at the counter of the State Store asking for Hennessy Cognac, or if funds were low, the cheaper Christian Brothers Brandy.

Two years later, on a rainy afternoon, Mom failed to navigate a curve, and crashed into an embankment. She proceeded to blame the auto mechanic for not having properly fixed the brakes. Again, an ambulance took her to the hospital. To keep money coming in during her hospital stay I visited her sales customers. To my surprise, I discovered I had the skill to convince people to purchase World Book. A customer even told me I was a perceptive person. Being bi-lingual, I had to look up the word perceptive in the dictionary. It would be another five years until I joined the World Book Company. It turned out to be one of the best decisions I ever made.

Beside health concerns of a bad back, weak stomach, and angina attacks, Mom also dealt with a painful knee. It was replaced at Geisinger Medical Center, but without success. An epidural anesthesia was used, and while half-awake she rambled in the operating room about the bears in our woods. While in the waiting room of the hospital, I despaired observing the suffering of people in failing health. The previous Sunday, the Schwab auditorium speaker at PSU focused on the scripture verse: *Faith is the substance of things hoped for, the evidence of things not seen.* I took great comfort from that recollection.

It was also the Easter season, and not a regular church attendee, I didn't know what the gray cross on peoples' foreheads meant. I asked a patient about this, and she described Ash Wednesday. The ashes of the palms of last year's Palm Sunday are used during a special church service. It is seen as a way to remind people of the need to repent of their sins. Was this something my mother needed to do?

11. POOR TIMES

Chicken necks and backs were our mainstay meal because they were cheap. Every imaginable combination of recipes was used. The best was fried chicken, with gravy made from the drippings and served with mashed potatoes. I can still hear the sizzling of the chicken pieces frying in the cast iron skillet. Jellied chicken loaf was also a regular meal, one that I grew to intensely dislike.

In front of our house stood a winter pear tree, and I discovered the joy of canning. Our basement shelves soon filled with jars of canned pears. It was a cold fall day when I brought from the basement empty jars to be washed, not realizing that one of them was cracked. As I immersed the jar into the hot water it broke slicing a nerve in my hand. The pain was unbearable, and I was so desperate for relief that I made a pact with God. If he took the pain away, I'd serve him forever. The pain eventually went away, and I tried to fulfill my end of the bargain.

One of Mom's piano students lived on a farm and occasionally gave us fresh green beans and potatoes. While picking beans in the field, the lady asked me about my future, and I replied I felt sure that in the next five years I'd meet the man of my dreams, and become a wife and mother. Little did I realize that it would take much longer.

My mother kept muttering, but I stopped listening, and only rarely replied. She didn't even notice. Still I managed to have some pleasant times for myself. I took sailing lessons at Stone Valley outside of Penn State, and eventually bought a used sailboat. Colyer Lake was a sixty-six-acre fishing lake not far from our house. Sundays were special, when I'd unlock the moored boat and head out with the wind. They were peaceful times as the wind and I worked together. The boat's name was "Selena," the moon goddess. Boaters waved as I serenely tacked back and forth across the lake. At least here I felt the satisfaction of going somewhere.

On a sunny afternoon, a lady in a canoe came up alongside my boat just as I was about to sail back across the lake. I noticed she was strikingly beautiful, with long blond hair, perhaps ten years older than my eighteen years. She introduced herself as the wife of one of my father's doctoral students, and her purpose was to encourage me to contact my father. He was back visiting in America.

She told me that she too had been the child of divorced parents, and had taken sides, something she deeply regretted. She also wanted to confirm that I had received the letter the certified from my father's lawyer. When our boats parted, I felt shaken and forlorn, yet I knew I couldn't be part of both of my parents' worlds. I couldn't bear the suffering my brother experienced. Walking home through the woods, in tears, I felt that my life would always be hard.

At the time I was too young to know about things like PTSD, Post-Traumatic Stress Syndrome. Psychologists today tell us some people who experience dire circumstances have severe depression or anxiety. Others have resilience or PTG, Post-Traumatic Growth. Looking back at my youth, this may explain the difference between my brother's and my reactions to trauma.

Refusing to let problems control my life, I took a pottery course in State College. Prior to using a potter's wheel, the wet clay had to be sliced, thrown, sliced again, and kneaded. It helped to ease my frustration before I went to my waitressing job. Satisfaction came as I enjoyed painting designs on the oven-fired pieces. Then it was exciting to enter several of my creations in the Penn State Arts Festival, the very first of its kind in 1967, and to find honorable mention ribbons on my pieces. The Festival continues to this day to be a popular annual attraction in State College.

One of Mom's piano client was a distributor for Bestline. A selling point was that the company's household and personal products were all biodegradable. This emphasis was becoming popular in an early attempt to protect water and soil from harmful chemicals. I liked the products, and signed up to be a representative. It wasn't hard to convince customers of the benefits. The company started around the time of Amway though they didn't last long as distributers ended up with cases and cases of products they couldn't sell.

Needing money was always an issue. Besides selling for Bestline, I joined a summer group that picked Crown Vetch from the fields. It was a perennial that had been brought from Europe in the 1950's, and planted along interstate highways. It was healthy work in fresh air and sunshine. We'd smile as passing cars honked while we were bent over, and sometimes waved back. After harvesting the plants, we packaged them on long tables in the barnyard. Under the noonday sun, the farmer's wife brought lemonade to go with our brown bag lunches. The farmer who employed me also fancied himself as an inventor. He had purchased World Book from my mother, and shown her his latest invention, a slinky card file. They visited factories with the hope they would be interested. However, this went nowhere, and the project died.

World Book awarded Mom a portable Singer sewing machine during a sales contest that year. Now my 4-H sewing skills could be put to use. I registered for a class in sewing and pattern designing. It was gratifying to say "I sewed this dress." I also tried to start a small business and approached a fabric store with my idea of sewing men's ties made with material selected by the customer. I named my business Ties by Li-Lo, but it lasted only a little while.

Occasionally we attended the Tussyville Union parish of a UCC and Lutheran church. While attending a woman's meeting, I talked with the speaker afterward, saying how impressed I was with her presentation. In the back of my mind I thought I'd like to do something like that. She was a manager at Danks & Co department store in State College. It was the beginning of the holiday season when I knocked at her office door, without an appointment. She recalled our conversation at church, and hired me on the spot for part-time work in the sewing department.

We were sometimes visited by members of the white clapboard Brethren in Christ church in the valley. If we weren't home or pretended not to be, they'd leave inspirational leaflets along with a Sunday bulletin. One leaflet called "Life is Too Short," was written by a religious writer stricken with cancer. It too became one of my mother's favorites. I was often perturbed as she quoted it in the company of friends.

> *Life is too short to ice cakes. Cakes are good without icing.*
> *Life is too short to eat factory baked bread.*
> *Life is too short to keep all your floors shiny.*
> *Life is too short to nurse grudges and hurt feelings.*
> *Life is too short to work in a room without windows.*

After another tirade of hers, I retreated to my room writing my version of the poem. However, it remained in my jewelry box under lock and key:

> *Life is too short for planting tulips. The fresh grass grows green.*
> *Life is too short for caring for dogs, when your daughter and son need you.*
> *Life is too short for being concerned about your status when everyone loves you.*
> *Life is too short for carrying resentments, when love is the reward of love.*

After eight years our push-button automatic Pontiac broke down, and left us standing by the side of the road. A friend of my brother's and a mechanic with his own business, suggested a station wagon that he knew for very little money. What he did not tell us was that the bottom of the car was rusted and held together by old license plates. Nevertheless, we bought it, and it somehow managed to get us around for a while.

The young family man was killed in a car accident not far from where he lived. He had failed to negotiate a sharp curve, and it was suspected that alcohol was involved. This was the same family that had a son in prison for the rape of a neighbor girl, and had younger son die of cancer. Pain and suffering surrounded many people in the valley.

The long-awaited trip to Germany was planned, and the house was rented to a graduate student and his wife. However, we didn't have passports or tickets. Before the new tenants arrived all of our personal belongings had to be stored in what we referred to as the piano room. It had a door separating a living/dining room that could be locked, and also a separate outside entrance. A fifteen-year-old neighbor boy helped us move all our stuff. I'd throw bags of clothes out the second-floor window as he caught them stuffing them in our car. He and I worked together with lightning speed to prepare the house.

To my mother's total surprise and shock, the couple, including a sheep dog, arrived with a moving van in the early evening. Mom thought they had rented our house furnished. Distressed we watched them unpack the van. Now all of our furniture had to be moved, and stored in the partially enclosed back porch.

We were without a roof over our heads. In a panic my mother called one of her friends who invited us to stay at their home for a few days, along with two of the dogs. It was early September, and night had fallen when we arrived at our temporary quarters, exhausted and completely drained. It was hard to believe what had just transpired.

The next day she contacted the owner of a log cabin used as a hunting lodge, and ironically not far from our now-rented home. It had electricity, but no running water or bathroom. Water for washing dishes and bathing was carried, in buckets, after walking a narrow path to the creek that ran alongside our new quarters. Drinking and cooking water was brought in from a spring close to our rented house. The cabin had not been used for a long time, the rent was cheap, but required cleaning and painting. By now I was an expert at both of these.

Winter soon arrived, and still no passports or tickets. Heating was from a wood stove in the kitchen and a cast iron coal heater in the living room. Nights were bitter cold as I'd wear a wool hat to bed to stay warm. To keep the fire going an alarm was set for 3:00 AM. It was like an unreal dream happening to someone else, as the once huge wood pile outside the house dwindled.

I could hardly wait for spring to arrive. I continued to work at my two jobs, now with chapped hands, elbows, and knees. I tried to keep my composure, never showing my true feelings. In some ways this was mild compared to what I knew my mother would be expecting from me when we got to Germany. I was terrified just thinking of this prospect. Even worse was what might happen if I told the truth of what really took place in our home.

The renters left as soon as the spring semester was over, and we moved out of the log cabin to return home. Now the plan was that the newly acquired tenants were to have the entire house except for the kitchen and piano room. The old galley kitchen was restored, and a noise canceling wall between what would be our kitchen and theirs was added. My mother slept in the piano room, and I in the kitchen on a roll away cot, except there was no space to roll it away. To get to the kitchen my mother went outside, and around the house. At times it was a treacherous challenge especially during winter months or when it rained.

The young couple were graduate students, and loved cooking with garlic. The forced air heating system sent the odors directly into our rooms. At least now it felt like I had my own apartment, if only at night, and I relished the quiet nights. Here I had heat from the furnace to keep me warm. Our bathroom was in the basement which was reached only from the outside. The toilet, sink, tub, and ceiling tiles were salvaged from a fraternity house slated to be demolished in State College. They were acquired with the assistance of our missionary friend and his old pickup. Wearing a kerchief to cover my hair, my job was to pull the tiles off of empty room ceilings.

Unfortunately, we still didn't have our passports or tickets to make the long-anticipated trip overseas. None of these rental arrangements proved to be an adequate solution, and work began this time to turn the upstairs of the house into an apartment complete with its own entrance and porch. What had once been my bedroom was turned into a kitchen. Trips again to kitchen outlet stores in the old truck commenced. The good news was that Mom would have people around her at all times after I left.

We finally had our passports and tickets in hand. Five suitcases were packed and ready to go, one solely for legal documents and law books. I can still see our thin friend straining under their weight as he lifted the heavy suitcase into his station wagon. Then he and his wife, my beloved six grade teacher, drove us to the Harrisburg train station for a direct train bound for New York City. We tipped the red cap porters handsomely until we arrived at the harbor.

Our ship was the SS France, at the time she was one of the fastest ocean liners in the world, and a handsome vessel. The voyage across the Atlantic took only six days. We docked in Bremerhaven after passengers disembarked earlier at Le Havre, France. The ship had been in service since 1961 and would soon be sold for shorter Caribbean cruises.

We could not afford an outside cabin with a window, they were reserved first class passengers, so we traveled with sixteen hundred tourist class passengers. This cabin, nevertheless, had all the luxuries I needed, a bathroom and shower. My mother finally relaxed as she eyed me with pride and satisfaction that she could offer this amazing trip. It was the first time I'd ever tasted a Honeydew melon. Its sweet taste still lingers in my mouth.

Arriving on the ship I wore a crisp navy suit, and to my pleasant surprise was mistaken for a ship stewardess. Schedules of upcoming events were posted in the cabin, and the next six days promised to be enjoyable. I had packed my best outfits, some my own creations, and others purchased at close-out racks.

During the orientation session we sat next to two charming young men, with whom my mother and I had lively conversations about life, the cosmos, and the universe. I was completely enthralled. They told us they were seminary students in Manhattan. With one student I spent the evening at a dinner dance, followed with a walk along the moonlit deck, and I found myself falling in love. I remember telling him that I sewed all my own clothes. When he asked if I sewed the dress I was wearing, I answered falsely trying to impress him. I still wonder if he noticed the tag on the neckline of my dress.

I quickly became aware, however, the other young man was keeping us apart. We did, however, exchange addresses before he departed in Le Havre. I waved goodbye to him from the ship's deck, hoping a relationship might develop. In my eagerness for this to happen, I had mailed a packet of religious literature about a historic church where Martin Luther had hidden in the 1500's, nearby to where we were staying. Unfortunately, I never received a reply, and wondered why.

At my grandmother's apartment in Germany, I mentioned to her friend that I had met someone from the western part of Pennsylvania, and was very interested in him. I went on to describe who he was, about his hometown, and his father's profession. To my shocked surprise she responded that she knew of him, her son had recently catered his wedding in America. I then knew why his friend had been so protective of him, he was already in a committed relationship.

Many years later, when I told my fiancée about this encounter, to my amazement he replied he knew the young men. They had been at General Seminary together, and he was aware that his classmate was going to meet his fiancée in England. I eventually learned that my shipmate heartthrob had been happily married with children, and served several parishes until his early death. The brief but lovely encounter could not have materialized into a relationship except in my imagination.

My mother now made trips to Germany by herself. A graduate student couple agreed to be caretakers of the property and the dogs. Again, the problem was when they arrived, she had not made arrangements for her trip. When she greeted the couple at the door, she proceeded to tell them the lawn needed mowing. They obliged, but when it came time for a shower, she said they couldn't use the shower in the basement because a black snack was in the tub. It would be three months later before she traveled to Germany.

The couple slept on a twin bed in the now completely enclosed porch room. The mattress was still from Germany, made of horsehair, and in three sections only slightly larger than a twin bed. During the couple's first night a mouse ran across the man's face. Long evening discussions with this graduate couple took place in the dim light of the living room. Years later, after Mom's stroke, they visited her, so strong was their relationship after all.

Mom now had the entire first floor. What had been the galley kitchen was turned into a bathroom by a friend visiting from Germany. Payment was that they lived at the house, and could use Mom's car for excursions. The only problem was once the couple left the toilet was clogged by a screw driver the friend had left in the drain pipe. The drain pipe ditch had to be reopened to extract the tool.

One by one our dogs died. For three of the four dogs it was my job to take them to the vet for the last time. Our most beloved dog had diabetes. Despite that the dog peed routinely under the grand piano, Mom wouldn't give her up, and she was given an insulin shot every morning. She died on the passenger seat of our car while I was driving to the vet. By now the house had a dank musty smell that lingered on the furniture and walls. So distinctive was the odor that our daughters often remarked on visiting other places "It smells just like Omi's house."

Again, renters were interviewed, and most turned out to be interesting. They too found my mother intriguing. A business undergraduate student rented her upstairs apartment during his final year at Penn State. I was not living at home by this time. But when I was visiting, we'd work together on the up-keep of the property. While we repainted the wooden fence, he bluntly told me that I wasn't marriage material. I was stunned, but wondered if he was right. I had overcompensated my loneliness with responsibilities. We kept in touch, and he became a successful businessman, who upon hearing of Mom's death, flew his private airplane to attend her service.

12. MOVING ON

Before the long-awaited trip to Germany, World Book approached me with a job offer as an area sales manager. Having observed how hard Mom worked, I didn't want do sales. Yet, on second thought, if I focused on management, I could turn meetings into positive teaching experiences. Ironically, my mother would be working for me.

The company manager visited, and asked what it would take to work for them. Half-jokingly I said if he'd offer a prize of a small chain saw, I'd join. We had just installed a wood burning Ben Franklin fireplace, had plenty of trees, but no chain saw. I made the quota, earned the chain saw, and was hooked. In addition to the chain saw, there was praise, a new feeling. When I signed the employment contract, I braved a step toward independence when I took my middle name of Barbara, distancing myself from my mother who had the same first name. I had grown tired of being referred to as little Lottie!

I inheriting a small team of representatives, and started running ads for new recruits in local newspapers. I'd meet with responders at town libraries and other locations, a few were good candidates, others not so much. Meetings and pep rallies were held before sales contest, and my team grew steadily. I was generous in time and attention, reaping benefits until I was promoted to higher level management. Returning from a meeting, my mother commented how she hardly recognized the person I had become. It was a bittersweet commentary, as I was still me. She knew who I was from the time I walked boldly, at age of five, to the table of the

Von Trapp family. However, conversations at home were rarely about me or what I thought or believed.

Meanwhile our car, with its floor held together by old license plates, gave up the ghost. A teacher friend took us to Big Valley to purchase a 1949 stick-shift Dodge. It was in good condition for being twenty-five years old, and again I swallowed my pride as I pulled up to the homes of customers. While working in an affluent neighborhood outside of State College, the husband told me that my car's spotlight was on. Spotlights were popular to see street signs and hidden driveways, even spotting deer at night. Embarrassed I discovered he was the owner of the local Audi dealership. He missed an opportunity, however, by not inviting me to his showroom. Shortly afterward I visited the family of the Saab dealer, and he sold me a used Saab. My next car would be a brand new company car!

The company headquarters assumed I had a seasoned sales representative in my mother, and gave me little training. Instead, I observed successful managers and modeled after them. The team soon became proficient in qualifying prospective customers as time was valuable. The company rule was it takes ten demonstrations to make one sale. With improved techniques, we brought it to one in every three demonstrations.

My collection of motivational books included "How to Win Friends and Influence People" by Dale Carnegie and "The Power of Positive Thinking" by Norman Vincent Peale. I would take these books and others on my six-month trip to Germany, studying and underlining valuable parts of chapters.

Back in the States, I took seriously Carnegie's theory that until one takes action everything is on hold, and nothing happens. Carnegie had created millionaires with this basic method even during the Depression. I understood that well, since my life had been on hold for such a long time. I had made the decision to join the company, and I was setting out to become the best I could be.

While driving to my counties I'd listen to motivational cassette tapes, such as "See You at the Top" by Zig Ziglar or "What Do You Really, Really Want" by Wayne Dyer. To be counted for a weekly sales contest, orders were collected and driven to the Harrisburg office at the close each contest. These late night "pony express" trips were pleasurable, as there was always food and fanfare at the office, though ninety miles away. I was having a particular bad day when in exasperation I asked my boss why my life was so difficult. He calmly sympathized and told me suffering is a common thread of life that happens to many people. Of course, he didn't know the full extent of it all.

The sales prospectus included poems that appealed to the emotions of a customer. Most of the poems spoke personally to me about what was missing in my childhood. It became my mission to remind parents that they were their child's first and most important teacher. In some homes I hope this may have initiated new paths for parents. "The Sculptor" hangs on my wall, and in the homes of our daughters:

I took a piece of plastic clay
And idly fashioned it, one day.
And as my fingers pressed it still, still
It moved and yielded to my will.

Then I took a piece of living clay
And gently formed it, day by day.
And molded with my power and art,
A young child's soft and yielding heart.

I came again when years were gone,
It was a man I looked upon.
He still that early impress bore,
And I could change it nevermore.

In stark contrast my mother never understood what happened to her son. She molded him into what he would become, and could not change it. When she'd declare we had a wonderful childhood, I could only turn away in utter disbelief. In everyday conversations with her I heard the phrase many times, "Everything comes to the light in the end." She'd say this with a glint in her eye directed at me, though I knew I was perfectly innocent. At such times I simply stood in astonishment. Her mental condition was so distorted I found it difficult to blame her too severely.

During the work week, I'd implement company procedures, as well as my own methods. Door prizes and awards were frequent at meetings, and we named my group the Sunshine Team. Unity, praise, teamwork, and achievement were emphasized. We practiced the four basic sales skills: know what you believe, tell it to your prospect, listen to what they believe, then guide them to close the sale. I was moving along, gaining confidence. Whatever prize was offered, I'd set a goal to achieve it.

At the branch office terms were used like, "top banana," "weekly sizzler." At one of my first branch meetings, and my first attempt at public speaking, I was asked to tell how I became successful. I boldly went to the podium and started my talk by saying "Let me tell you the first time I sizzled." The entire room broke out in laughter, and I blushed not realizing the connotation of what I had just said. When the room grew quiet again, I continued with my theory about success.

The World Book Company soon became the longed-for family. I was important to them, and received admiration for who I was. They became the aunts, uncles, and cousins I never really had. The training was also like the college education I never had the opportunity to obtain. At a sales conference, a company zone manager spoke of her philosophy of raising children, saying, "There are two lasting gifts we can give our children, roots and wings." Since I missed these, I decided this was going to be my motto for my family. Later at a bookstore in Germany I discovered the quote is from the great German philosopher Johann Wolfgang von Goethe, many of whose books ironically were in our home.

It was during the experiences in a variety of homes that I consciously decided, how I would or would not someday raise my own children. Many times, I had to stay composed as I observed parents use negative words like "you're so ornery," "you're bad," "don't touch that," or "don't bother me," during my visits with them. The result was that the children responded with even more negativity. Calmly, I'd hand the little people my children's books, and smile as the astonished parents observed their child's interest. It became a selling point as the youngsters calmed down.

A few of my favorite statements during presentations were: "you are your child's first and most important teacher" "twenty years from now no one will remember what furniture you had in your home, but they'll see the results of your home in your grown children." These emotional phrases, combined with an excellent product, helped to make a sale. Most customers were friendly and pleasant to be with. At one home, after I gave a choice of which binding they'd prefer, I casually said "Why don't we go ahead and do it" to which the man laughingly said "Fine with me, you pay half and I'll pay half."

Commissions grew steadily, and now I could buy stylish clothes. Nevertheless, I complained to my manager that I was stressed. He replied that stress is what we put on ourselves. To my surprise he also told me I worked better under stress. Still, I never completely bought his assessment, thinking to myself what did he know about my stress. During a conversation with a Mall manager concerning space at one of her events, she expressed how much she admired that I was a strong woman. I quietly thought, if she only knew what I'd gone through to get to this point.

During my sales tenure in the 70's and 80's, I had only one unpleasant experience with a customer. I was engaged in a pleasant conversation with the lady of the house, when her husband walked in. She introduced me, and he went into another room. Shortly thereafter, he came back telling me in a harsh voice it was time for me to leave. He then escorted me to the door while reprimanding me. His wife had told me he was an ROTC instructor at Penn State, apparently used to giving orders. I was shaken but determined that he won't have the upper hand and walked across the street to another customer, hoping no one was home. No one was there, and I scampered to my car in tears.

By this time, I had been promoted to district manager. I would be training a former social studies teacher, and the son-in-law of a local school superintendent. We worked well together as I learned management skills. As with anything in life, work is more enjoyable and productive when humor is present. A manager once told me when two people are laughing together, they are never far apart. I'd treated my trainee to lunch finishing my coke in the car. As we pulled into the driveway of our prospect's house, he made an amusing comment, and I started laughing so hard the drink came out of my nose, running down my lips. It was so embarrassing that we left quickly. He would go on to take my position in the company, when I was promoted two years later.

Two recent college graduates were also assigned to me. We'd meet at the restaurant where I'd once waitressed, the employees remembered me, and were happy for my success. There we laid out our strategy as well as field training schedules. The young men were six years younger than I, full of energy and frivolity. During that year I felt I'd returned to the lost days of my youth with them. For my birthday, they surprised me with a gerbil and cage because they didn't want me to be alone. It was a happy year; my mother was away in Germany, caring for her mother.

At the Atlanta International Achievement Conference, we heard a VP tell the audience how she had put her son through law school. At that moment, my trainee leaned over to me, and whispered he decided to go to law school. Not long afterward I received a letter of gratitude for the life lessons he had learned while working with me. He went on to become a successful attorney in a metropolitan city.

The other young man moved south continuing his career in finance. We saw each other numerous times as I'd travel to out of state conferences. While still with the company our friendship was such that he drove me to the nearest Immigration and Naturalization office in Philadelphia. I was now in my late twenties, yet my permanent resident card showed my picture as a five-year-old. Having earned a trip to Acapulco, I feared I wouldn't make it back into the country with the outdated picture. With trepidation I approached the INS official, fearing they may have a huge file on me or my family. It was not the case, and I breathed a sigh of relief as I walked out that sunny day with a brand-new card. The card still had the same status that was of such concern to my mother, the official just shrugged his shoulders when I inquired what it meant. Mom never knew I made this trip.

It was a warm spring day when I knocked on the door of a referred prospects home in Lemont. I introduced myself as calling on families with children, asking if I could come in. The lady of the house was a stylish, beautiful woman who asked me a few questions, and then explained that presently she had guests, but would I please come back. To my surprise she said she wanted to learn the art of selling. This had never happened to me before, and I felt like skipping to my car with joy. She, I discovered later had small children, was beginning a MBA program at Penn State, and had always been intrigued how to positively influence people. I hired her, she was successful, and years later was my maid of honor at our wedding.

I soon decided I was tired of being lonely. One of my college student customers during my days of waitressing was now a married man with children and a university professorship. We had a chance meeting, at the Weiss Market in State College, in my quest to use a telephone for a car shop to change a flat tire. I became a friend of the family, and ask my friend and his wife if they'd introduce me to one of his students. Not long after my request, I was invited for dinner along with a graduate student, and a relationship quickly developed. For the first time I did not have to have a secret romance.

My boyfriend was working on his doctorate degree, I became his mentor and encourager, and he became mine as we tried to understand each other's family issues. He lived off-campus, and we sometimes stayed at his place after a late date. Other times we'd spend the day sailing, and he'd stay at my place. When my mother's evangelical minister friend paid an unexpected visit, he didn't grimace when he saw my boyfriend's travel bag in the house. Though his beliefs were different from what I was accustomed to, the minister remained a good friend.

Later that summer we visited my boyfriend's family home in the western part of the state. They welcomed me warmly, but I was saddened by the fact that his parents were divorced. My dream was to belong to a traditional family. Meanwhile, my mother was suspiciously having his handwriting analyzed in Germany, and of course sent me only the negative findings. He went on to become a full professor at a university in the south.

It had been ten years since my brother left for Germany, and life had not been kind to him. He could not stop his pain with alcohol and drugs. I flew to Germany visiting him in the German state-run institution outside of Munich, and was appalled at what was happening to him. With trepidation, I agreed that he could come and live with me. It had been fourteen years since he left Pennsylvania for California with only a few of trips back to see us. I was uncertain if I could cope, especially since my mother was remaining in Germany to take care of her aging mother. In my search for a solution I found a Christian organization that was willing to work with me. They offered him a place to stay while we got to know each other again.

I nervously waited in the PAN AM terminal of JFK airport for my brother's arrival. He was one of the last ones to depart the plane. I could tell immediately he was nervous; anxiety was written all over his face. Once he saw me his pained expression eased, and we made our way to downtown Manhattan, and the iconic New Yorker hotel. The next morning, we had Amtrak tickets to Harrisburg.

Before my boyfriend and I parted he helped me with my brother's living situation, and we made several trips together to make the arrangements. Though I realized by then that we were not meant for each other, and told him so, he remained helpful to me. As our connecting train from Philadelphia pulled into the station in Harrisburg, I was relieved to see him waiting there. After the three of us spent quality time together, we dropped my brother off at the place he'd be staying. Driving home my boyfriend pulled to the side of the road while I vomited.

My brother's living situation at the religious facility wasn't working out. Reciting Bible verses was not sufficient for someone with his background and problems. In getting to know my brother again, I realized he was very depressed, but also the same good-natured brother I knew as a child. He moved into our house with me. Fortunately, a graduate student tenant upstairs would often talk to him while I was working. It was hard to maintain a positive disposition, fulfill my work as a sales manager, and also try to help him. Fearing that his mental problems would be looked down on, we traveled great distances to seek professional help. Nothing seemed to work, and I was often exasperated.

Friends tried to assist me as best they could. Some were appalled at what I had undertaken. That was when I leaned on the song by the Hollies:

> *The road is long*
> *With many a winding turn*
> *That leads us to who knows where*
> *Who knows where*
> *But I'm strong*
> *Strong enough to carry him*
> *He ain't heavy, he's my brother*

A friend asked me if it had ever occurred to me that perhaps my brother was not capable of changing. Her comment gave me pause but it didn't sink in until years later. Others would tell me I was only fooling myself, and wasn't dealing with reality. He suffered from nightmares, and a deep sense of guilt. He kept saying that orphanages could have been built with the money the German government spent on him while in the mental institution. It was heartbreaking. He also had an annoying habit of pulling out his hair. To occupy his time, he read through the entire set of the World Book encyclopedia.

Mom returned to America on Christmas Day. I began to wonder if Christmas was jinxed for us. My grandmother's hotel was bombed on Christmas, my father left for America during the Christmas season, and now I dreaded the return of our mother into our dysfunctional home on Christmas Day. On the way to Dulles airport to pick her up, I urged my brother that his hair pulling habit would irritate and anger Mom, and he'd be wise if he stopped. To my great amazement, while driving home that day, he stopped his habit and never did it again. We wanted also to be especially considerate towards Mom, as her mother passed away at ninety-eight while she was caring for her in Germany.

At home our living situation was again difficult, we had only two main rooms plus the kitchen. Again, I set up my cot under the picture window in the kitchen, and my brother slept on a sofa bed in front of the fireplace. His depression turned to anger, now his turn to have the tirades toward our mother. While I was at a sales conference at the Hershey Hotel, I received a phone call that my brother was in the hospital with a severely broken arm. He later admitted it was a good thing he fell as he had harbored angry thoughts of harming Mom. The universe once again intervened.

It was at the same conference that I received another call that a good friend and colleague had taken his life. I was devastated with the news having spent a week skiing with him and his friends that winter. I remembered riding the lift with him when he asked me whether I ever felt like a phony. Other than this remark he did not give an indication of the seriousness of his depressive moods. He was one of the most engaging people in our group. At a previous sales conference in Chicago he took my arm and said,

"Let's meet Marshall Field Jr," the president of our company then, which we did!

His circle of friends was again younger than I. My friend had shared some of his troubled childhood with me, he had been deserted by his mother as a baby. I met his father and step-mother, and they seemed like reserved New Englanders. He knew my brother was struggling with his past, and when I was informed that he had been hospitalized for depression, phone calls and letters ensued hoping to encourage him.

With my last letter I tried to assure him he could pull himself out of this dark place. The letter was found after his death, in a snow pile in front of his mailbox, unopened. Not fully aware of his deep depression, the hospital gave him a pass to leave for the weekend. He asked his father for money, bought a full tank of gas, and returned to his recently purchased home, with the car idling in the garage. Though I was fond of him, our relationship wasn't a romantic one. I knew then why it hadn't developed into one.

My brother's hospital stay was lengthy, he wore a half-body cast with his arm raised over his head. While in the hospital he was visited by another Christian college group with eccentric views, and they invited him to come live with them. It was a bittersweet as he again had to swallow his convictions. The students had considered this their mission, and also undoubtedly to have a new recruit.

He slowly recovered, and my brother never came home again. His life would involve various apartment rentals and odd jobs. At one assignment his manic episodes returned when he started drinking. During an episode he was in the midst of washing animal cages for a research lab on the PSU campus when he forgot to take the cat out of the cage, and it went through the industrial washer. He hadn't meant to harm the cat, days of anguish and guilt feelings followed. My mother was mostly out of the picture, traveling back and forth to Germany. I was left to manage his moves, pay for, and clean his apartments whenever he was told to leave.

Easter that year was particularly warm and sunny as we picked up my brother for Sunday brunch in a restaurant. Soon his agitation toward my mother escalated, and we quickly left the restaurant as customers looked at us in bewilderment. He calmed down momentarily, and we took a scenic drive in the countryside. What followed could have been a scene out of a movie. I knew we were in trouble when he lit two cigarettes at the same time. I stopped the car, he jumped out shouting loudly while flapping his arms pretending to fly. My mother was screaming as I ran into a house to call 911; he was in danger of hurting himself and others.

This would be the first of many trips to visit him in a psych ward of a hospital in Danville, Pennsylvania. He improved while on medication, but only momentarily, as he would resume drinking and lose himself in the lost years of his life. I knew why this was happening, and had deep empathy for him. The refrain *he's not heavy, he's my brother* kept me going. My father was now out of the picture. He'd requested no further contact with my brother after institutionalizing him in Germany.

The episodes didn't let up, and I was now well-known to the drug intervention offices in town. They were always helpful, and at times we'd spend hours monitoring him, as he couldn't be committed until he became a danger to himself, others, or was damaging property. His last episode lasted until 3:00 am, when my brother tried to beat down the door of the Phyrst, a well-known bar in State College. An ironic aspect was that the street address was also the number of my mother's P.O. mailbox. An ambulance was called, and he again spent four weeks at the State Hospital.

Needing to do things for myself, I took a ski club membership at the then called Skimont outside of Boalsburg, and befriended a school teacher. Besides skiing we both liked taking walks, and soon became walking partners. He was good-looking, kind, and single. We planned a trip together to the shore, but at the last minute he informed me that his young friend would be coming along. I also discovered that he suffered from health-related panic attacks. I'd reserved two rooms at the bed and breakfast I had frequented over the years, but cancelled his when he booked a room for himself close to the local hospital. In frustration I bought an outrageously overpriced leather handbag from a boardwalk vendor, racking it up to shopping therapy.

On a company trip to Hawaii, I met a young man again younger than myself. His parents held high level management positions. We had a great time driving around in his rented convertible, stopping at beautiful beaches, and at one point getting caught in a riptide. He was from the southwest, and a skier. We made arrangements to go skiing together in Pennsylvania. It was a bitterly cold day when I picked him up at the airport near my northern-most territory, and close to a ski area. He was indeed a good skier, and despite the weather we had some nice skiing.

I was to meet him after my South West sales conference. Before leaving my mother suggested I should follow up on what he told me about himself. By now, she no longer felt the need to end my relationships. At first, I laughed at her warning, but something led me to make a phone call to the place of business he told me he owned. When I asked to speak him, the response was there was no one there by that name. In disbelief I had fallen for his lies, I ended the relationship. By now I was stunned at my failed attempts at companionship.

13. HAPPY DAYS

My zone manager visited my territory to offer me an advancement with the company. I drove through what was to be part of my territory in Allentown, Pennsylvania allowing the feel of the area guide me in my decision. I knew it was time to move on, yet the location did not seem right, and I declined. My quotas continued to be met and my team grew. As representatives came and went, I'd receive cards and even gifts of thankfulness for our time together.

That year at the New Orleans sales conference, my submitted entry for the conference theme and logo "Learning is Forever" was chosen. However, later a VP apologized that they failed to publicly give me credit. In between sessions, I was called to the private suite of the president of the company. When I entered the room and saw my smiling zone manager, I knew I'd be given a greater opportunity, and I'd better take it. I was ready, the location was perfect, and I accepted immediately. My new home would be Lancaster, Pennsylvania.

It was summer and business was slow when I scheduled a flight to Germany to inform my mother I was moving. To my great surprise she had no objections, because now she needed a place to house her Biedermeier antique furniture that had been in storage for thirty years. Her old house was cramped and not big enough for all of it. The German mover was notified and some of the shipping labels were changed to my new apartment. Perhaps my guardian angel was at it again.

Before my trip, I drove to the new territory to give a dinner speech for my new team. I considered carefully what to say and what to wear. I wanted to appear gracious yet not too business-like, so I dressed smartly but with warmth and humility. I would have three male fulltime managers reporting to me, one resigned because he expected to have the position, and wasn't going to work for a woman.

I concluded my remarks that evening in the beautiful atrium of the Eden Resort in Lancaster with Walt Disney's favorite lines.

> *Think…of the values and the principles that you are going to live by.*
> *Believe…in yourself based on the thinking that you have done based on the values and the principles that you are going to live by.*
> *Dream…about thinking what you want to be based on the belief in yourself which is based on the thinking you have done about the values and the principles that you are going to live by.*
> *Dare…dare to make your dream a reality, based on the thinking you have done about the values and the principles that you are going to live by.*

The next day, one of my representatives offered to help me find an apartment. She invited me to her home for a luncheon along with her recently retired minister. During the conversation it became apparent her minister had an unmarried son, and as he suggested, would love to meet me. In a straight-forward manner I asked if he had a photo. He showed me a picture taken during his son's seminary years in Manhattan. The expression on his face was that of a serious young man, and I was not entirely impressed. I went on to hire the retired minister; little did I know ten months later my world would never be the same.

I packed my clothes and possessions, including my newly acquired cat to keep me company. Mitzer sat curled on my lap during the two-hour trip. As we made our way across the mountains into the flat terrain of my new location, I saw a beautiful rainbow before me. To me it was a sign of promise that all would be well.

The antique furniture arrived at a port in New York where a moving van waited to transport seven pieces to my address before continuing to Mom's address with the remainder of the shipment. My apartment was on the second floor, and accessed by an elevator from the open lobby. The final piece was a valuable wardrobe used by monks in 1825 at a cloister. It wouldn't fit into the elevator, and the movers informed me that a hoist would be needed. I quickly calculated that this would be a costly expenditure. A phrase I heard many times from Mom was *probieren geht uber studierin, to try is better than to study.* The wardrobe had an indentation at the top and the elevator had an indentation at the bottom. I told the movers to turn the piece upside down, and voila it fit.

Just before I moved, my brother and I were notified that our father had died. I deeply regretted not having contacted him when he was gravely ill. I was still bitter that we children suffered so much, and perhaps placed unwarranted blame on him for abandoning me. At night, alone in my room, I wept for him and the daughter he never really got to know. Now it was even more important for me to succeed, and make my father proud.

My team, along with other divisions, were invited to a holiday dinner at the famous Hotel Hershey. My future father-in-law brought his wife who eyed me with great interest and admiration. I thought nothing of it at the time. She was a stately, well-spoken lady, and I liked her immediately.

I bought my first Christmas tree along with German/European ornaments, and tried to enjoy my new-found and hard-fought freedom. A bonus in the apartment was a lovely screened-in porch and a cozy fireplace. At night the glowing wood embers reminded me of the struggle to keep warm in my youth. With each delivery of firewood, I thanked my lucky stars for bringing me this far.

Lancaster also had many unique antique shops. In one I found a framed picture of the well-known *"Desiderata."* Some of my favorite lines are:

Go placidly amid the noise and haste,

As far as possible without surrender
Be on good terms with all persons.
Speak your truth quietly and clearly.

Avoid loud and aggressive persons,
they are vexations to the spirit.
If you compare yourself with others,
you may become vain and bitter;
Be yourself.

You are a child of the universe
no less than the trees and the stars;
you have a right to be here.
And whether or not it is clear to you,
no doubt the universe is unfolding as it should.

With all its sham, drudgery, and broken dreams,
it is still a beautiful world.
Be cheerful.
Strive to be happy.

Whenever I felt discouraged, which happened frequently, I'd pause, look at the picture, take a couple deep breaths, and continue my work. It seemed the sentiments were ideally suited for me. When my work quotas seemed unattainable, I'd recall the words attributed to both Francis of Assisi and Martin Luther "Even if I knew that tomorrow the world would end, I would keep hoeing my garden."

The company was good to me, and for me. There were trips to Acapulco, Hawaii, Lake Placid Winter Olympics, and Italy. In Italy I would be traveling alone on a tour, an unsettling thought. In Milan we toured the famous multi-spired cathedral. There, while purchasing postcards, I wasn't aware I was being watched by a family of gypsies. Suddenly a piece of cardboard was pushed against my chest. I sensed I had been robbed, and they disappeared like scattered mice.

Our next stop was a mountain resort where I wandered the narrow cobblestone streets, and bought a pair of ski boots communicating by sign language. What I failed to consider was I'd have to carry the boots throughout Italy. That night I remembered the warning my mother said to be careful where to keep money, and that a safe place was under my pillow. The problem was the next morning, I forgot to take the traveler's checks from under the pillow. Now I had zero funds!

In Florence, besides retrieving my traveler's checks, I visited with my mother's friend when they were in their late twenties. She spoke broken English but enough to tell me what a charming woman my mother had been. She described the friends they had during this time. One was a Medici, a distant relative of the famous Lorenzo de' Medici, and ruler of Florence from 1513 to 1519. Another was related to the family that owned the Fiat Company, and a Countess, with whom my mother played violin duets. I relished the awareness that my mom had accumulated these special memories. It reminded me of something she often said "Memories will someday be of great importance."

At our final stop in Rome, I threw two coins in the Trevi Fountain, recalling the Sinatra song "*Three Coins in the Fountain*." I had only two wishes, one to arrive safely back in the States, and the other to find my soulmate. Looking back, it worked!

Days and nights found me discouraged at being single, and upset at the unfairness of my life. While at a training seminar with a colleague, we stopped at a bookstore where I bought a book "*How to Find Someone to Love*." Several months later, this colleague and I were hosts at a dinner for teachers interested in part-time summer sales jobs.

My future father-in-law brought his English teacher son to the meeting. I was flushed from scurrying around placing flowers on the tables, as they arrived early. The young man gave me a warm smile, and I was completely disarmed. During my presentation he listened to every word I said, nodding in agreement, seemingly interested in both my speech and myself. During dinner I nudged my colleague, and whispered "I think he's the one I've been waiting for."

Earlier that spring at an antique store on the Jersey shore boardwalk, I found a framed German illustration, "Nur Einen," meaning "Only One," and later presented it to my husband-to-be.

> *I only need one who will go with me*
> *Through light and shadows,*
> *Through happiness and pain.*
> *I only need one who understands me.*
> *I only need one who is concerned for me,*
> *Is kind to me, and who speaks love to me.*

In return he gave me an autobiography of Liv Ullman, the Norwegian actress, called "Changes," with her photo on the cover. On the title page he wrote:

"I bought this book to look at the picture. I put it up on my shelf next to the "Nur Einen." It reminds me of you, and since I don't have a picture of you, I got the next best thing. It has been my companion this week. She looks like you, though you are narrower and sharper in feature, and that much more attractive to me. It also reminds me of your many other qualities – affectionate tenderness, European knowingness, and natural intelligence. It's very easy for me to think of you and do nice things for you. I will always care for you, and fill up all the little gaps and corners of your life. Keep me in your heart always as I do you."

My future husband took the training class with eagerness and enthusiasm. Our first date was to his high school reunion. The relationship progressed quickly as I took him to my parental home. He told me of his ambitions for the future as we sailed on the lake. In State College we attended the annual Arts festival. Later that evening, as we sat by lake, he whispered he wanted me to be the mother of his children. I suspected a marriage proposal might be imminent! Two weeks later, as we returned from a date, we parked in the driveway of my old home, and I asked him if he had a question for me. It was then he proposed, and I accepted in a heartbeat.

Like the words of the song that my fiancée sang to me, we felt that our time had arrived. Not only had I been searching for someone to share life's journey, but he had been also.

Like a river flows
Surely to the sea,
Darling so it goes
Some things are meant to be.
Take my hand,
Take my whole life too,
For I can't help falling in love with you.

Meanwhile, my brother and I were notified about my father's will. He had left everything to his second wife, and we were not mentioned in the will or the newspaper obituary, a terrible rejection. The German government, however, had a law stipulating that children of the deceased would receive a small percentage of any monies not part of the designated will.

My brother's life continued to be difficult, even after several hospitalizations. He refused to give up alcohol, which for him was worse than drugs. Only when drinking did he feel confidence in himself or so it seemed. I continued to loan him money. Once we knew the German funds were coming, I began noting my brother's loans with his understanding that they would be deducted from his small inheritance.

His mania increased, and I feared that he'd waste the inheritance, or worse buy a gun, and I began to fear him. His love-hate relationship toward our mother was unwavering, and his dependency on me a burden. I had to be less involved so I could have a life of my own. My fiancée and I consulted with a lawyer to have a letter written informing my brother he had used up his funds. The letter also suggested it was time for him to stand on his own, and make a life for himself. What ensued were years of hatred directed at us. It was a trying time, yet my fiancée remained at my side, even though his parents expressed concern about my family situation.

During the next twenty years of estrangement from my brother, he was often homeless, sleeping under bridges or in parks. On numerous occasions, and in desperation, my mother contacted the Salvation Army in cities from where he called us collect. They'd find him bringing him to shelter for food and a place to sleep. To this day, I am generous when I pass a holiday bell ringer at stores, always with a lump in my throat of gratitude and sadness. He was desperate to be a recipient of SSI, Supplemental Security Income, for people with disabilities. Months and even years were spent as he fought the system. When at last it was approved, he received several years of back funds, and was off to Europe.

In the beautiful city of Prague he met a nice woman with whom he lived for the next half year, until the night he had a vivid nightmare in half-sleep and hit her. Returning to the States, he made his domicile in the Clearwater, Florida area, sitting in classes for free at the University of South Florida. There he had some decent years as a beach bum, with his own small apartment, until our mother's death sent him into a tailspin. It was here and with the help of Jewish Family Services that I stepped in, forging a relationship with him during his last fifteen years.

14. CELEBRATIONS

Our summer wedding was ideal. We were married in the Penn State University Chapel at University Park, where my father had taught, my husband graduated, and my parental home was nearby. My mother and I found a wedding dress in the quaint town of Boalsburg. It was made to order for me, at least in my mind. The cost for the dress and reception for seventy-five people was one thousand dollars. The dress was traditional, with a scoped neckline, bridal train, and pointed sleeves at the wrist. I wore my long hair in a French twist with a comb of pearls attached to a veil. A strand of pearls along with earrings from my high school prom completed my attire.

I had gone to my mother's house a few days before the wedding. Instead of relaxing, I'd spread delivered gravel around in the courtyard in preparation for guests, who never came. My mother was forever preparing for visitors, like Miss Havisham in "Great Expectations" or Amanda in "The Glass Menagerie."

Wholesale roses had been ordered, and it was arranged for my fiancée and his best man to pick them up. The florist was considerably out of their way, and they were issued a speeding ticket trying to make it on time for the rehearsal. With the fine of the ticket went any savings we hoped to achieve with the less expensive roses. My mother and I were still the ones late for the event.

Our rehearsal dinner in the Allen Room, above the well-known Corner Room in State College, was memorable. We stayed overnight in a downtown hotel, I with my maid of honor, and he with his best man.

For me the night was one of reflection on my past and future, and didn't allow for much sleep. As morning came, I peered out the window to see my future husband sitting on the edge of the hotel swimming pool looking up at my window. His wave gave me the confidence I needed for the day.

It was a hot July day as my husband's father presided at the ceremony, and my future sister-in-law played Pachelbel's "Canon in D" and "Trumpet Voluntary" by Purcell as well as the traditional Wedding March by Wagner. My fiancée and I walked down the aisle together, meaningful for us as we were going into this marriage as a couple. I was awestruck seeing the beaming faces, my lips quivering with emotion. As I passed my mother, she gave me a slight smile signifying "you're doing fine." Standing before my misty-eyed father-in-law, peace came over me, and I was ready for the ceremony to begin.

My husband had composed a marriage litany for the group reading:

> *Happiness in marriage does not just happen; it is created and cultivated.*
> *It is the making the pilgrimage of life together.*
> *It is the gratitude for both the great and small gifts in this world.*
> *It is the placing of persons above position, property, or possessions.*
> *It is learning how to forgive.*
> *It is holding one another's well-being on a level with our own.*
> *It is doing for one another as we would want them to do for us.*
> *It is becoming totally open with one another.*
> *It is becoming a friend as well as a helpmate.*
> *It is not taking ourselves too seriously but having a sense of humor.*
> *It is seeing ourselves as others see us.*
> *It is listening as well as talking, giving as well as receiving.*
> *It is realizing that no man is an island unto himself.*
> *It is not being afraid to disagree; it is the sharing of inner feelings.*
> *It is knowing that perfect love casts out fear.*
> *Happiness in marriage is not only marrying the right partner, but also being the right partner.*

It would be my father-in-law's two hundredth wedding, yet he was so moved that when it came to the part where he asked who gives this woman to be married to this man, he reversed it "who gives this man to be married to this woman." Mom had been coached the evening before to say, "I do," which she promptly did. When it came time for the vows, I had to quietly remind my father-in-law of the words. It was an emotional time for everyone.

To my delight, as we departed the building, we met the next couple who were to be married right after us. She had been a colleague at my first waitressing job, and now a financially struggling graduate student. We offered to leave the candles and ivy which they happily accepted. As we left the chapel, I smiled as I heard the familiar refrain of the wedding march and saw our lit candles glowing through the windows.

The wedding reception was held at the stately Nittany Lion Inn. We used the rose filled vases that had adorned the altar and windows of the chapel for table decorations. Later my husband and I presented the vases to the special people in our lives. A formal favorite wedding photo was of the two of us standing by the white pillars of the Inn, just like Rhett Butler and Scarlet O'Hara. We actually weren't quite like them; the photographer was paid with a set of encyclopedias.

During the reception, toasts were made by many friends and family, a judge, professor, doctor, as well as others. My sister-in-law read the poem "Love Song" that my husband had written. Years later the same poem was read at the weddings of both our daughters.

It is the oldest and the newest of things,
It is the most common and most precious of things,
It is the most universal and most personal of things,
Every human being knows it or will know it
Yet it happens to everyone as if for the first time.
It is fragile and yet most powerful,
It is invisible but everywhere present.

Life is planted, grows and blossoms in it
Yet we can spend a lifetime without it.
The glow of love is in all eyes.
The glow of love is on their faces,
The glow of love is in our hearts,
It is the essence of things.

My brother was not at the wedding. In May he'd come east to see our mother, but with the tension that existed we both decided it was best that he not attend. I missed my witty brother I had grown up with so many years before. Nevertheless, I was actually grateful he and I were not closer. It allowed me to handle the heartache of his life in a somewhat detached manner.

Our honeymoon on the Chesapeake Bay was modest, just like we wanted, time to ourselves without stress. As I considered my future, it seemed I was surrounded by kindness, not only from my husband but also his family. This was the life I had always hoped for.

That fall my husband responded to a request from a church seeking a youth minister. We liked the congregation, somewhat between my upbringing and his preparation. I was happy as this was the first time I belonged to a congregation. I recall the moment a member asked me to make something for a bake sale. I felt honored to be asked, and became more involved.

By January 1982 I knew I was expecting. We were overjoyed, yet aware that children weren't allowed in our apartment building. My husband sent out applications for both teaching and ministry. To supplement our income, he traveled on weekends to a small town outside of Bedford, Pennsylvania. I often accompanied him on these trips, staying with a family who were members of the congregation. We liked them, and they liked us. An application was submitted, and we were accepted as their full-time minister and wife.

That August I bid farewell to my team and my World Book colleagues. I was ready to begin a new phase of my life, that of mother-hood. On September 2 we welcomed our beautiful first daughter into the world. We stayed in the hospital for only twenty-four hours. She was an easy-going little person who loved being with people, even strangers. She was just three weeks old when we moved to our new home. The congregation was delighted to have a young family in the parsonage.

I was contented being a mother first and a minister's wife second. I feared I might become too involved; the arrival of our daughter was an answer to that prayer. My mother-in-law became my mentor and friend, giving tips on how to be happy in my new role. One of her best suggestions was to accept, with gratitude, any gift offered, even if it was a bag of potatoes and we had a pantry full of them. She had retired as a teacher and minister's wife after fifty years.

I had only one request of my mother-in-law, a hand-made calligraphy drawing of the poem *"Children Learn What They Live"* for our baby's room. I knew my mother hadn't intended to hurt me but had failed on many of these points. As I'd read the lines, I vowed to be a good mother, and learn as much as I could about raising children.

If children live with criticism, they learn to condemn.
If children live with hostility, they learn to fight.
If children live with fear, they learn to be apprehensive.
If children live with shame, they learn to feel guilty.
If children live with encouragement, they learn confidence.
If children live with tolerance, they learn patience.
If children live with praise, they learn appreciation.
If children live with acceptance, they learn to love.
If children live with approval, they learn to like themselves.
If children live with recognition, they learn it is good to have a goal.

I had always wanted to sing in a choir, and now was my opportunity. Inviting members to our home was an aspect of our ministry. Choir members were sent invitations for dessert at the parsonage, and I served Baked Alaskan, a fancy and difficult dessert. I quickly realized it was a mistake when the guests just stared at my confection. Apple pie and ice cream would have been a better choice. Each day was a new learning experience.

One of our members was a fifteen-year-old young girl from a working-class background. She loved coming to our house as a mother's helper. Not having had a close relationship with my brother, I was irritated that this young girl seemed to be always at my heels. The morning lesson during church service was "whatever you do for the least of these you do unto me," and I was ashamed how I felt toward this girl. Another time during Sunday school class, the teacher reminded us that we didn't always have to like everyone but were compelled to love them. This changed my outlook, and I began to better accept her and others.

That winter we had the first of many parsonage Christmas parties. I spent free time baking, including a German Stollen, a family tradition during the holiday season. Though it took our girls years to actually like it, I relished each slice, along with memories that came with the smell of baking. Christmas Eve, the church was decorated with a beautiful Christmas tree and candles that glowed in the windows. I and others read sections of the nativity story. After reading *"Mary treasured all these things, pondering them in her heart,"* I left the podium teary eyed. I had been through so much during the first half of my life, and felt grateful as I pondered my bittersweet memories.

It was a brisk fall day as my husband and I drove to the Immigration and Naturalization Service office in Pittsburgh in preparation to become a naturalized citizen. I had studied the literature, but again felt anxious that something derogatory might be noted in my file. When I again asked this official what the status on the permanent resident card had meant, he replied it had no negative meaning, just a symbol used at the time. I walked away shaking my head in disbelief for the years of pain this irrelevant symbol had caused my brother, father, mother, and myself.

The interviewer proceeded to ask questions about my background, character, and willingness to take an oath of allegiance to the United States. Other requirements for citizenship included residency, knowledge of the English language, U.S. civics, and pledge to the nation and the Constitution. The civics section did not come easy for me, but I passed!

Several weeks later, my husband and his parents, along with our one-year old daughter made the trip again to Pittsburgh. In the courtroom our little girl waved the American flag I'd been given as I read the oath along with three hundred soon to be American citizens.

"I hereby declare, on oath, that I absolutely and entirely renounce and abjure all allegiance and fidelity to any foreign prince, potentate, state, or sovereignty, of whom or which I have heretofore been a subject or citizen; that I will support and defend the Constitution and laws of the United States of America against all enemies, foreign and domestic; that I will bear true faith and allegiance to the same; that I will bear arms on behalf of the United States when required by the law; that I will perform noncombatant service in the Armed Forces of the United States when required by the law; that I will perform work of national importance under civilian direction when required by the law; and that I take this obligation freely, without any mental reservation or purpose of evasion; so help me God."

After being sworn in, I had my ears pierced and my hair cut that very same week. It was official, the United States was my home. I now had roots and a family that loved me.

We were leaders in our community, and my husband's church was well-respected. Each year on World Day of Prayer, the local churches came together to hold a service. It had been poorly attended in the past and this year the materials hadn't arrived on time. Several young women and I attended planning sessions. There I presented the idea of focusing on

Healthy Parenting and Families. We continued the theme of child rearing practices for the next three years, and filled up the pews each year. Community soloist added to the event. I was again on a mission to help moms and dads understand the importance of parenting.

The following are excerpts from my presentations:

In the lobby of the church is a wall hanging that reads, 'A child is the only known substance from which an adult can be made.' I'd like to take it a step further and add a responsible world can be made. Allow me to illustrate this by the story of a father and his young son who were spending an evening together. The father was at his desk preparing the budget and bills as his young son attempted to get his attention. Being pre-occupied the father said to wait a little longer. Soon he became aware that he had to come up with something to occupy the little boy.

On his desk was a magazine whose cover held a picture of the world. Tearing the page out the father cut the picture into a puzzle, giving his son the pieces with some scotch tape, hoping this would keep his son busy until he was finished with his work. Within minutes his son returned with the world perfectly taped together. In astonishment he asked his son how he did that so fast. The boy replied, "Well, you see, Dad, on the other side was a picture of a little boy, and I figured if I put the boy together the world would turn out okay too.

It is by no means an easy task to understand what a child needs. We don't always realize that a child is sensitive to the environment around him. Just as a plant grows and thrives in the sunlight but withers in the biting wind, a child can only develop to the fullest in a cheerful, happy, and positive atmosphere. They tell us that half of what a child needs to function as an adult is absorbed in the first five years of life. As early as three months a baby responds to rhythm. Without rhythm how can he acquire poise, grace, and confidence?

The following poem is about the brief time we have with our children:

To My Grown-Up Son

My hands were busy through the day, I didn't have much time to play the little games you asked me to, I didn't have much time for you.

I'd wash your clothes; I'd sew and cook, but when you'd bring your picture book and ask me, please, to share your fun, I'd say, "A little later, son."

I'd tuck you in all safe at night, and hear your prayers, turn out the light. Then tiptoe softly to the door, I wished I'd stayed a minute more.

For life is short, and years rush past, A little boy grows up so fast, no longer is he at your side, his precious moments to confide.

The picture books are put away, there are no children's games to play, no goodnight kiss, no prayers to hear, that all belongs to yesteryear.

My hands once busy now lie still, days are long and hard to fill, I wish I might go back and do the little things you asked me to.

Our daughter was a year and a half, and we had another one on the way, as I presented my second talk the following year:

The problem with parenting is that by the time you're experienced you are unemployed. I recently read a quote, those are wise in child rearing who open their arms more often then they open their mouths. As parents we tend to nag too much, give too many directions, and not enough praise and reassurance.

Parenting begins with an expectant mother who is carrying her child. It is interesting to note that when we prepare for the first child, we gather all the material things needed, often forgetting the mental and emotional needs to be met in the early years of a child's life.

One of my favorite and most meaningful quotes is, "Train up a child in the way he should go, and when he is old, he will not depart from it." Every child has a unique destiny to fulfill, and it is our privilege to raise our children not simply in the way that any and every child should go, but in the unique way he or she should go. The following letter was written by a young man, whose parents, never having been trained to be their children's first and foremost teacher, missed participating in the crucial years of child raising.

Dear Folks,

Thank you for everything, but I 'm going to Chicago to try to start a new life, you ask why I did those things that gave you so much trouble, the answer is an easy one for me to give you, but I'm wondering if you'll understand. Remember when I was six or seven and I wanted you to listen to me? I remember all the nice gifts you bought me for my birthday and Christmas, and I was really happy with them for about a week. I really didn't want presents, I wanted time for you to listen to me like I was somebody who felt things too. Because I can remember even when I was very young, I felt things, but you were always so busy. Mom, you were a wonderful cook and you had everything so clean and were always tired doing all the things that made you busy. But you know I would have liked crackers and peanut butter just as well.

If my sister ever has children, I hope you'll tell her to pay attention to the one that doesn't smile a lot because that one will be crying inside. I think the kids who are doing all the things that the grown-ups are tearing their hair out worrying about, are really kids looking for so somebody that will listen to them.

If you folks had ever said to me, pardon me, when you interrupted me, I'd have dropped dead. If anybody asks where I'm at, tell them I went looking for someone with time, because I've got a lot of things I'd like to talk about.

Love, Your Son

At my last presentation, our children were two years old and six months old:

A lady once told her friend that my husband and I started out with seven theories and no children and now we have seven children and no theories!" That is about where my husband and I are now too. But the truth is that as parents we need to have a sense of direction. One of the most important components or principles in raising healthy and happy children is to have a loving marriage. Norman Vincent Peale in his famous book "The Power of Positive Thinking," related that his wife held to the conviction that the number one career between motherhood and wife was that of a wife as children need to experience the love of both parents in a united front.

Another principle is that parents be open and honest with their children. Putting up a front and pretending to be virtuous in a way that no one really is, usually doesn't work. Children see through this, in other wards be real. To be able to admit our mistakes and to say I am sorry is always an appropriate thing to do, even if it is hard. There are times we may sometimes punish our children in anger and not for the sake of the child. They are sometimes being punished because at that very moment they appear to be a nuisance."

The third principle is that discipline should be for the good of the child, and not for the convenience of the parent. The function of discipline is that we enter into an agreement with our children to help them use freedom wisely. It's been said that too much attention for bad behavior can lead to even more bad behavior to get attention. Discipline from a parent is really the child's way of learning self-control. When punishment is called for, it is the wise parent who carries it out in a reasonable fashion, and also keeps their word.

The fourth principle is called 'unconditional love,' or 'positive regard.' If our love for our children is based solely on what they do for us or what they bring to us in the way of satisfaction, then it is not real love. A child owes us nothing but love. One child counselor stated that his definition of healthy parenting is what I do for my children is payment I make to the future for the debt I owe the past.

My own family situation, however, didn't change very much. My mother continued to make trips to Germany, and I'd make the three-hour drive, now with babies, to assist her. Other times we'd bring her to stay with us for several days.

During our final year with this congregation I often saw a scrawny ten-year-old boy downtown. After a shopping trip he helped unload my groceries, and soon started coming to our house after school where I gave him healthy snacks. He enjoyed playing with our girls, and I liked his being there until the day we noticed our collection of silver dollars was missing. Our church president took delight in giving them to our girls throughout the year. Then a sizable check made out to a charity was gone. Lastly, a foot-high piggybank in my husband's office was taken.

I was devastated as we asked the young boy if he had taken these things, his mother came with him, and they denied it all. I knew he had stolen from us, and felt a deep sense of betrayal. Especially painful was I had just suggested to my husband that we could help him get out of poverty by perhaps adopting him. It was the beginning of our wanting to leave the area, I felt violated and hurt.

That summer we vacationed at the Country Inn of Berkeley Springs WV. My husband had to spend a night at a church conference some distance away. We enjoyed restful days, and befriended a couple with whom we shared parenting stories, and I told them I was in my first trimester of pregnancy. They offered to watch our nine-month-old as we went out to see the movie "Gandhi," about one of our peace heroes.

The next day the couple left to go home, and my husband left for the conference. During the night, and all alone, I was awakened by cramps, and spent the next hours between our room and the bathroom. Our nine-month-old daughter slept through the night. In the morning, I made sure I had breakfast, and fed our little girl her oatmeal, all the while fearing what had happened during the night. In tears I called my mother-in-law, telling her I thought I'd lost our baby. Then I calmly asked the desk clerk to call a taxi to take me to the nearest hospital. They personally drove me to the emergency room where doctors confirmed that I had miscarried. There was no way to contact my husband, and waited alone for his return that evening. It was apparent that this pregnancy had come too early after giving birth the previous year.

Back home I enjoyed the quiet community, serving on the Board of Health at our local clinic. Each day we'd stroll with our daughter to the merchants in town and the post office, greeting people by name. Once again in January I knew another baby was on the way. This was different, I felt healthy and strong. Little did we know that a tragedy was looming.

In August 1984, after a pleasant visit from our in-laws, our little family took a welcomed nap. We were abruptly awakened by blaring sirens. Looking out the upstairs window, in horror, we saw cars without drivers floating down the street carried by torrents of water. It was surrealistic as we quickly moved our books to safety before the flood reached our doorstep.

The rescue squad insisted that we leave for higher ground. My husband refused as I was eight months pregnant, and the water might be contaminated. We watched with relief as the flood waters ceased rising just short of our porch. It had been raining for days and the creek coming down the mountainside was swollen. At a curve the force was so fierce that it broke the river bank, sweeping away a small business and killing all five of its employees, before devastating the center of town.

Our church was miraculously untouched by the flood, and became headquarters for many organizations that came to the town's aid. Relief workers slept in the church's social room on cots and sleeping bags, and were fed by the women of our church, taking showers and doing their laundry at our home. The parsonage was practically attached to the church. The town looked like a war zone for many weeks, as clean-up crews worked to restore normality.

We had made close friends during the three years we were there, including a couple in their sixties without children, who became honorary grandparents. On a warm night in September they took our two-year-old daughter to their home when I was in labor. The nearest hospital was sixteen miles away. Our adorable baby daughter made her appearance in the early hours of the morning. However, this sweet child wasn't always happy when I'd leave her sight. But I always knew she'd be a resourceful one, as she'd pull herself together once I'd leave her eyesight.

My husband had made a large hand-drawn sign "It's a girl!" for our porch to the delight of the town. His mother arrived to stay with our older daughter while we were in the hospital for a night. To my disappointment she stayed only a few days leaving us to figure out the parenting rituals on our own now with two children. After she left, I was touched emotionally when a poor neighborhood young woman with little children, not a member of our congregation, knocked at our door with a casserole of baked beans and hot dogs. It was the tastiest casserole given with kindness and thoughtfulness.

At the birth of both our daughters, they never left our sight, something I had insisted on with the doctors. This practice was just becoming popular, and the nurses were not always eager to oblige. Years later I found an article in a parenting magazine: *When it comes to the hours and days after having a baby, some new moms want their babies close by in the hospital room, not leaving their sight. Doctors and administrators began telling new mothers that unless it's urgent, the baby should stay with them. The main objective of this new protocol is to encourage moms to breastfeed and bond with their newborns by staying together, in the same room, around the clock.* We were ahead of our time!

I began singing the Brahms Lullaby in German to them, a custom that continues with our granddaughters. I was always glad our girls never asked me to translate the lyrics as the third line was rather morbid, "tomorrow morning, if God wills, you'll awaken again."

Guten Abend, gute Nacht, Mit Rosen bedacht,
Mit Naeglein besteckt, schlupf unter die Deck'

Morgen frueh, wenn Gott will, wirst du wieder geweckt

Morgen frueh, wenn Gott will, wirst du wieder geweckt

Guten Abend, gute Nacht, Von Englein bewacht

Die zeigen im Traum, dir Christkindleins Baum

Schlaf nun selig und suess, Schau im Traum's Paradies

The American version is gentler.

Lullaby and goodnight, with roses bedight

with lilies o'er spread is baby's wee bed

Lay thee down now and rest, may thy slumber be blessed

Lay thee down now and rest, may thy slumber be blessed

Lullaby and goodnight, thy mother's delight

Bright angels beside my darling abide

They will guard thee at rest, thou shalt wake on my breast

My husband's work involved three churches in three communities, and we looked forward to having one congregation in one place. He placed his name in the search process, and we chose a church not far from where my mother lived. She was in Germany at the time, and I felt a deep dread about being just over the mountain from my difficult past. I didn't listen to my feelings, and we accepted the position. The new church graciously covered the costs of our move including the onerous job of packing. To our younger daughter's dismay, the movers packed a chair on which her favorite teddy was sitting. Tears were shed and it was another learning experience.

We were again in a large parsonage, and our children had a backyard to play in. My husband and a friend built a fence so that I could watch the children without worry as they played in the homemade sandbox, and on a swing set moved from our previous location. The backyard also became home to two pet rabbits in a self-constructed bunny pen. These were idyllic days in many ways. As with my childhood, make believe dress-up was a favorite pastime of our daughters. On our tenth wedding anniversary

I divided my wedding veil and gave half to each as they paraded around as brides.

For their September birthdays I sewed long play dresses for our girls. We delighted as they turned moving boxes into a post office and general store. My husband's wish that they learn to play independently and creatively was happening. We also made lots of playdough, and during a play date the little girl said "My Mom won't make playdough because it's too messy." To me child's play, even when messy, is their work.

The church grew rapidly as young couples were drawn to the friendly atmosphere, and to an active Sunday school where plays and programs were held. I was asked to teach second grade. We brought with us varied experiences that came with working with many kinds of people. In one instance, the first-grade teacher was exasperated by an older member who kept disrupting her class to record attendance. This had been an issue for years, and no one knew what to do. I suggested that the intruding member be given her own desk in another room complete with a desk nameplate. Now everyone was happy.

I again organized the Community Bible School, rotating with other churches and their facilities. Children and teachers came with smiles on their faces eager to participate. It was a chance to use my organizational skills honed from working with my sales representatives. A favorite theme was: *They that wait upon the Lord shall renew their strength, they shall mount up with wings as eagles, they shall run and not be weary, and they shall walk and not faint.* It reminded me of my own hard-fought pilgrimage, and of how I managed to go on. My husband was always encouraging and supportive of these activities.

My mother returned from Germany on a fall day, the day I stopped sleeping. I intuitively knew it was a big mistake to be just twelve miles from her. I was so exhausted from not sleeping that I had to quit teaching Sunday School. An appointment with our family doctor was made, and the first thing he said as I tearfully told him that I couldn't sleep was "you are not crazy, you'll be alright." An anti-depressant was prescribed and it worked for a while.

The anxiety of not knowing when she'd call with her endless requests was overwhelming. We naively thought she'd recognize that a move to an apartment would be the best thing. I eventually realized she was not capable of making such a decision, especially with all of her possessions. She rarely threw anything away, TV dinner tray, cottage cheese container, or receipt. I felt her leaving the house would only happen on a stretcher, which was the case years later.

Our daughters went to Nursery School in a neighboring town. Upon visiting the town's elementary school where our oldest would attend Kindergarten that fall, I was dismayed that the school didn't have a playground, and the classrooms were bare of any beauty. We, therefore, enrolled our daughter in a private religious school that had blooming geraniums lining the classroom windows. The following year when our second daughter was to start school, and given the high cost of private school, we made peace with our idealism, and both attended the local public school.

That summer we were invited to a North Carolina beach house with my husband's extended family. Our younger daughter was the shy one who would cry when I left the room, something she did from birth on. It was apparent that my mother-in-law was displeased, as she prided herself in never having cried, and always coping as a child. It was not a comfortable feeling when she asked to speak to me in private, telling me that something was amiss in my child-rearing practice. I had been criticized constantly in my parental home, and this did not suit me well. My husband was supportive and took my side, knowing that our daughters' mannerisms were the result of heredity and not just training.

On our way home, we stopped at a restaurant in the Outer Banks that promoted a time-share facility. We took the tour, were given a cheap movie camera for our time, a dinner at the facility's restaurant, and bought a week of ownership. I was overjoyed by the idea that our vacations would be just for our family with a bedroom for each girl, and a kitchen overlooking the playground and pool area. It was a relief to think we would have a place where we wouldn't be criticized, and it could be paid for with profit-sharing from my company. It turned out to be exactly the same amount of money.

Our first vacation at the new resort was however dampened by the news of Black Friday, 1987, when the stock market fell in value. We were new investors, and had just moved our small combined savings into high yield junk bonds at the suggestion of a broker. Nervously watching TV, while our girls colored in their coloring books, we realized that we had lost a portion of our savings. However, we celebrated the fact that we had invested in this vacation time-share, and did not lose those funds. It was an eerie feeling of not being in control.

As it turned out, this investment had an even higher yield, ensuring that we took family vacations every year. Finally using a point system allowed for multiple vacations in a year. A favorite destination at the time was the Poconos, only an hour away. Other times we did exchanges to Vermont, Montreal, Williamsburg, Rhode Island and even Germany on several occasions.

Back home along with a new neighbor, whose husband was a business executive, we presented a plan to the PTA to purchase playground equipment and have a work party to construct it. It seemed unhealthy to us not to offer children playground equipment during recess and after school play. Refreshments at PTA meetings were now served on fancy tablecloths with silver tea and coffee servers and flowers. Attendance and interest at the meetings increased dramatically.

Both our girls were taking piano lessons, their teacher was a kind, and thoughtful person who took a strong liking to our family. After five years in the community it became apparent that we needed to move on in search of a better school system. I worried who would assist my mother, when the girl's piano teacher offered to be the contact person, and visited her once a week.

In our search for a cosmopolitan community we had two congregations that wanted us to accept their offer. While on a get-a-way retreat, something we often did through the years, we made our choice based on the location of the parsonage, library, community pool, and excellent schools of Livingston, New Jersey. The new congregation welcomed us warmly and we knew that this place would see our daughters through their school years. We would be close to New York City, where my husband had spent three years at General Seminary an added bonus in getting around Manhattan. Church members generously gave us tickets to concerts at Carnegie Hall, Lincoln Center, and the Paper Mill Playhouse in Short Hills.

I had become too involved in the previous parish, and after counseling, decided I wouldn't repeat this pattern. I was supportive of my husband's work, attended social groups, sang in the choir, but held no official positions. I remembered a friend saying she resented being a preacher's kid because her parents were never home in the evening.

We were in a community of varied people, and valued them. Prior to accepting this pastorate, my husband and I had a meeting with his supervisor. This gentleman had two high achieving daughters both studying to be doctors. I asked him the secret of good parenting. He replied "Celebrate both the big and little occasions of life." This became our motto throughout the years, and now with our granddaughters.

In a quest to figure out who I was, and how my youth had been affected, my husband and I attended various workshops. Many popular speakers had concepts like "dysfunctional family," "toxic shame," and "inner child." Each event brought some new clarity. The best response from a therapist to my question of why had this happened "It was a tragedy" was his reply. It was the first time I felt some peace about my painful past.

In most tragedies no one person is to blame and it involves the entire family. In literature it is a drama in which the main character suffers, the result of a tragic flaw, and inability to cope with circumstances. This spoke directly to my life. Mom had been impacted by the catastrophe and persecution of war, and like many others was still a casualty. There was also the atmosphere of living under Nazi dictatorship, which was in the air that was breathed.

Another seminar included a three-day workshop at Omega Institute. An exercise was to write a letter to my mother as if a little child, and a second letter from her back to me.

Dear Mom,

I was really frightened when I was little, fearing that you didn't love me because I wasn't mean to my father.

I was upset that you didn't understand your problems of anxiety and suspicion, and that you didn't seek help. I didn't know much about mental illness then but I knew you had a problem, and that it was not my or my brother's fault. You had so many good qualities. I wanted so much to have a family that cares, helps, and trusts each other. A family that did everyday normal things. I missed not having had a youth, with friends and boyfriends who you would accept and welcome.

I was always afraid someone would find out about your problems and then what would I do? There was no one to go to, I was all alone, and very afraid of you. I tried to do my best to help where I could. I did all the housework and did it well, yet you always found something to criticize. You made me feel like I couldn't do anything right.

I deeply regret that I didn't have the strength to bypass you to see my father and be the daughter I should have been. To be proud of him and his accomplishments, and he of me and my accomplishments. Simply to be with him as he grew older, talking and listening to each other.

I am sorry for the times I was snippy, and at times cold as the years went by, but I was only trying to tell you how hurt I was.

Love, Your Daughter

Dear Daughter,

I wish things would have been different, I had so many plans and ideas of what I wanted, but somehow everything always went wrong. I would get so upset, and couldn't cope well. I know I hurt you, I blamed you to cover the shame of my illness. I tried to hide it as best I could, and I am truly sorry for the suffering this caused both you and your brother.

I made the trips to historical landmarks with you to show you that I wanted to offer you more out of life. I always knew you were my sunshine. You were such a beautiful baby, and I admired your proud forehead and pretty ears as you grew, neither of which I had.

Thank you for all your love and the many ways you reached out to me throughout my life. I understood your reasons for being snippy to me, and regret that I could never admit I had a problem and tell you that I was sorry I hurt you with my unkind words and mixed up thoughts.

Love, Your Mom

There, I finally said how hurt I was, and she said she was sorry! My husband became my close confidante and counselor. He, in turn, attended lectures and retreats by noted spiritual and other leaders. We even took a course in hypnotism in New Your City, hoping to bring back memories from my past. My husband tried to understand my need of caring for my mother and brother. There were no easy answers to explain this, given all that had happened. We both eventually came to the conclusion that it was probably also a German trait of dedication I had inherited.

My mother suffered a stroke at her home, and was found by our children's former piano teacher. Her schedule was to come Thursdays, but that week she came on Tuesday, and saw my mother through a window lying unconscious on the floor. Mom's upstairs tenant was home, and they found a window that could be opened. After been airlifted to a larger hospital and diagnosed with minimal chance of recovery it was apparent that she would never go home again. Plans were made for her care, and for her burial needs when the time came. It was her wish to return to her homeland in

Germany upon her death. Even after a second stroke she lived for another six years in a nursing home.

That spring I wrote a letter to my brother:

I haven't had an update on our mother since I left last Thursday. Our phone bill is beyond what is manageable. They know to call me with any changes in her condition. Now that the crisis is over, I realize there is nothing more I can do. She has the best care available. For a woman who was so negative, her condition now makes her appear to be like someone else. I have to admit I had a difficult time staying at her bedside.

I never experienced much talking with Mom, she always dominated the conversation. Now I read and sing to her while I am there. I don't resent her anymore, but regret that she never sought professional help for her delusions and fears. It has been only recently that I fully realized she had deep psychological problems completely unrelated to our father, you, or me. What is most distressing is that she could have been helped, if only she had asked for it.

We have been hurt. I will not allow these family patterns to affect my children, and dedicate this desire to our late father. I have sought counseling to figure this out, and it has helped. Let us not honor her abusive ways by continuing the patterns of the past.

Love, Your Sister

It was a difficult time for our family, with trips to see my mother at nursing homes in State College, Milesburg, and Bellefonte. I'd invariably pull away with tears in my eyes. My in-laws were often worried about me, and would remind me to take care of myself. I'd turn away quickly while saying goodbye to them so they wouldn't see my pained face. The burden of what lay ahead of me was heavy.

However, in time our visits were fairly pleasant, especially when she could no longer speak. I'd sing German Folk songs and she sometimes sang along, an ability that lingered for a few years. Now, blaming me, or making me feel guilty for not staying longer, was no longer the case. She knew I was there, and sometimes stroked my hand. After years of anguish, I finally felt comfortable around her. Our daughters often came along and we'd stay at friends' homes. The girls painted Mom's fingernails while I'd cut her hair. She allowed no one else to do this, and became agitated at the staff if an attempt was made. When we visited as a family, we treated ourselves to a stay at a hotel with an indoor pool.

15. HORIZONS

Our family of four made the trip across the ocean during summer vacation. My mother's family owned a small property that could be sold with the funds used to pay for her nursing facility. We started in London, traveling with a Eurail pass to Brussels, Rhineland, Paris, Munich, and a pilgrimage to the institute of psychologist C. G. Jung in Switzerland, an idol of my husband. Our young daughters were good travelers as we stayed in several youth hostels over the three-week trip.

Before the trip I had found the address of my father's long-time friend in Germany. Letters were exchanged and we met for lunch in Munich. I didn't even know where my father's grave was located. This distinguished professor and fellow scientist, like my father, was rightly skeptical of my seemingly renewed interest in my father. It was only near the end of the visit when my emotions surfaced that he realized how deeply sorry I was. I also made a phone call to my father's lawyer concerning perpetual care for the grave, and he too was suspicious of my interest. Little did I realize that later this lawyer's wife's grave would eventually lead me to my father's godson and his family.

After returning to the States it was time for me to branch out from family concerns and resume work. Coupon shopping was a favorite pastime of mine, and I considered becoming a personal shopper. After placing a fancy ad in our town newspaper, The West Essex Tribune, I attended my first book group discussion at the Livingston Library hosted by the director. While listening to her speak of her goals to make the library "user friendly" and a place to gather and meet for discussions, I felt led to tell her I agreed with everything she said and would like to help toward that goal. She looked at me in astonishment and gave me her business card, requesting that I make an appointment with her later that week. As no one responded to my being a personal shopper the idea was dropped.

In the meantime, I took our girls, now eleven and nine, to find a less expensive nursing home for Mom. This was not an easy task to accomplish, yet with the help of staff and a friend, I convinced her we were only taking a drive in the country. Instead we drove to a nursing home with the lovely name "Whispering Pines." What she didn't know was that all had been arranged, and her suitcase was in the trunk. This new place was one third the cost and in a chalet setting. Granted it also had some colorful staff people who didn't mince words around their clients, but nevertheless she relished sitting on the deck outside of her little room. Winter came, and life changed for her as she worried incessantly about her pipes freezing at home. I received the call that she had another stroke, this time taking her speech as well as her walking ability.

Several weeks passed before I went back to the library. I accidently ran into the director and she enthusiastically said she wanted to hire me immediately. The town's dynamics were changing and the population was becoming more diverse. The circulation desk at the time was in an awkward location and customers sometimes were visibly frowned upon for things like late fees. A turnstile at the entrance was uncomfortable and awkward as people made their way through it. For several weeks I was trained for my new job by long-time employees, some not exactly happy I was there, fearing I might take their job. To remedy this situation, I made a point of acknowledging them with compliments or a flower on special occasions.

When I started working at the library, I was told a professional architect had been hired to design a new check-out desk and location. After being there for several weeks and watching the customer flow, it occurred to me a new area was not what was needed. The entrance to the main section of the library was across from an old circulation desk and cluttered work space, and was the first impression for town residents. The checkout desk simply needed to be moved to the other side of the large room.

Now when customers arrived, their view would be of a lovely slate tiled lobby with doors that opened to a portico and newly installed benches. Prior to my plans the lobby and doors to the outside were blocked by the circulation desk, filing cabinets, typewriters, and tables piled high with books. To my surprise the professional architect's design was rejected, and mine chosen.

Our library was part of a state wide library system, and an award was being offered for the most creative and innovative new library concept. A group of forward-looking employees, including myself, proposed a concierge like desk right where customers walked in. A large antique, once a check-out desk, was brought up from the bowels of the basement, and the Help Desk became a reality.

Though we did not win the prize. I spent my part-time hours at this desk, answering the phones and questions, registering new customers, and directing people to the correct department. My most important job, however, was to be welcoming as I greeted customers. In time circulation statistics increased, and the library became a renewed center of the community. Oddly enough in my youth, I had often observed how unfriendly receptionists were, it was then my interest in customer service piqued, and I vowed to make a difference.

My personal approach was rewarded in many ways, as expressed in a letter among others sent to the library trustees from a patron:

Dear Board of Trustees,

I want to comment and commend Ms. Barbara Long who is "stationed" at the Help Desk, a hot spot of activity.

Time after time I hear Ms. Long answer the phone in such a nice, soft, courteous manner. And I have noted the warm friendly way she handles help requests. Very comforting.

Just thought you would like to know and appreciate a nice person; a professional employee, an asset, and a lady.

Sincerely, A Patron

The town mayor and council welcomed new residents each year with a catered affair. The year we moved into town a charming resident greeted the gathered group and spoke to the audience. I leaned over to my husband and whispered I'd like to get to know her, she's so vivacious and positive.

This same lady stopped at the library Help Desk, and I told her about the impression she had made on me. We immediately became not only good friends but I served on many of the committees she headed, even becoming a chairperson myself. Much of my people skills I honed from her. I treasured her thank you note to me after working with her during the annual "Youth Appreciation Week."

"Before the week is over, I have to write my "Barbara Appreciation" note. Not only do you keep everything moving forward, your positive attitude makes no task impossible to achieve. You are truly a blessing in my life. We are going to be friends forever, and to know that is a joy in my heart. Thank you is not enough, but I give it with respect, admiration and love."

With the help of a travel agent we planned a train trip across United States. I had fond memories of trains as a child, and we wanted to offer our daughters new experiences. As a toddler and on an overnight Pullman train, I poked my foot out from the curtained compartment, and said, "Mr. Pullman, please tie my shoe." Apparently, I thought he was supposed to do everything we asked.

We packed lightly, each girl had a backpack and small suitcase. Our older daughter was entering high school and the younger one middle school. We knew the time was approaching when such adventures might not be possible or enjoyable. Taking a southern route our first stop-over was Atlanta. While my husband visited Martin Luther King's birthplace, the girls and I enjoyed Atlanta's Underground and swimming in the hotel pool. Our next stop was New Orleans. Just prior to arriving my husband and our older daughter fretted about the trip, she cried over missing her friends, and he complained about the amount of time the trip would take. After a relaxing Steamboat Ride up the Mississippi with a jazz band, they both wanted the trip to go on.

We celebrated my fiftieth birthday in San Antonio on the famous River Walk, complete with a red rose and a mariachi band serenading me thanks to my husband. He also surprised me with a Saint Barbara charm and necklace. It was at the Alamo that our girls learned their father had a favorite Davy Crockett coonskin cap as a young boy. The next day we were back on the train heading for Tucson.

The temperature reached 113 degrees as we scampered between our timeshare unit and the pool during that week. In the coolness of the evenings we ventured out and saw the Julia Roberts movie "My Best Friend's Wedding." From Tucson we rented a car headed for the Grand Canyon. Our first sight of the canyon at sunset took our breath away. The next day we didn't trust the donkeys' knowledge of the narrow trails, and we walked halfway down into the canyon with water bottles hanging around our waist.

In Tucson we waited for the much-delayed train, and were informed that a young girl had been struck and killed trying to chase her dog off the tracks. We spent the night on the hard benches of the train station. To the girls' dismay the delay resulted in our having to cancel a visit to Disneyland, but we did enjoy a stopover to see my husband's nephew in Los Angeles. We found ourselves mesmerized by the changing landscape, and spent much of the time in the glass-domed lounge. There our younger girl worked diligently on a scrap book of the places we visited.

From Denver to Chicago was a two-day ride, and a sleeping compartment was reserved. Dining car reservations were made each day, with elegant and tasty food served on linen tablecloths. Our train car, however, had problems with the air-conditioning and septic system. The conductor gave us the welcomed news that we'd receive a full refund. Our daughter was about to tell the conductor that it wasn't too bad, when I nudged her to be quiet. By that time, they both knew a nudge from us meant serious business.

In Chicago we visited the Merchandise Mart Plaza which encompasses two city blocks and at one time the home office of World Book, then known as Field Enterprises. While I was with World Book, in the seventies and eighties, they occupied an entire floor. The Windy City offered us time to stretch our legs, walk out on the Steel Pier, and ride the enormous Ferris Wheel. Our unforgettable three-week journey was nearing an end.

Living in a parsonage took diligence and patience. In our last church home, the family room was in dire need of new carpeting. When I inquired if it would be possible for the carpet to be replaced, one board member replied "do you see it in the budget." However, I had a back-up. My mother-in-law, who had found herself in similar situations, gave us a monetary gift for the new rug.

Our garage had an old-fashioned door that had to be manually lifted. In winter this was difficult, and we purchased a discounted garage door opener, asking if my husband could install it. A board member replied they were not paying my husband to be a garage door installer, and sent his professional electrician to install it.

We were happy with the leaders and the congregation, parties and get-togethers were frequent and enjoyed by all. When the book "It Takes a Village" by Hillary Clinton, came out I agreed with her theme. Our daughters were in the company of people who truly appreciated them. They in turn became self-resourceful young women.

Each year in New Jersey, we housed an American Field Service student on their way to live with a host family for the year, and again when leaving for home. It was an interesting experience for our elementary aged daughters. It was with interested curiosity that they could spent time with these young people, and later when they were in high school, they continued their interest in other cultures.

The young people were with us for only a short time, yet it gave us the opportunity to take them to historical places like Thomas Edison's laboratory, Ellis Island, and the Statue of Liberty. Some of the students were anxious at first about their upcoming experience, and others shed tears when leaving the United States. We were there to soften these anxieties.

Both of our daughters worked at baby-sitting jobs after school to help defray the cost of high-end clothes. They started as young as twelve being mothers' helper after school and on weekends. We were relieved that they were aware we could not afford everything they wanted, and for the most part were content. Both girls attended their Jewish friends' Bar or Bat Mitzvahs. Our community was mostly Jewish and Catholic, with only a small population of Protestants or other religious groups. Not knowing the customary amount expected as a gift, I embarrassed our older daughter at her first invitation when the gift she gave was that of an everyday present as opposed to the customary sizable monetary gift.

When it was apparent that our younger social butterfly daughter would be attending over twenty bat mitzvah ceremonies, and reality set in about the cost of the events for us. Many were lavish affairs such as the trip to see the "Lion King," on Broadway that included transportation in air-conditioned buses. Shopping for fancy dresses was now in order, something I enjoyed doing with our daughters. They knew to start first at the sale rack before looking elsewhere. Sometimes we found dresses marked down even at high end stores. On several occasions my husband and I were invited to attend both the ceremony in a synagogue, and the reception at a hotel or country club.

During high school both girls held steady summer jobs, and chauffeuring began in earnest. One girl was a life guard at Camp Horizon, the other was a teacher's aide at Little Learner's. Our life guard daughter came home from working, stating that she knew for sure we had raised both her and her sister well. She explained that her charges at the camp pool hovered around her, unlike the other camp counselors, because she remained sweet and kind even when the children were a challenge. From our younger daughter's employer, we heard excellent reports about her strong work ethic and willingness to help wherever needed. They both were proud of their earnings, and would split the cost with me for their party clothes and gift checks.

To earn extra income, I joined Welcome Wagon. It was one of the first all-women companies in the US. As a Welcome Wagon hostess, I visited new homeowners with a gift basket of samples, coupons, and advertising from contributing Livingston businesses. Home visits continued for over 50 years until 1998, when changing demographics meant fewer homeowners were at home.

In the process, not only did we find our family dentist and other professionals, but some became close friends. Our younger daughter's first employer, Little Learner's, was one of my newcomer customers. When I returned with our daughter to inquire if they were in need of summer help, she was hired immediately. She remained working for them even during college breaks for the next seven years.

By now, it was apparent that the home in the woods needed to be sold, in order to keep paying for Mom's care. Before this every German antique piece of furniture was sold, even her Steinway grand piano went for a fraction of its value. I was informed that the piano needed $10,000 of repairs, something we couldn't afford nor did we have the space for this large instrument. I kept her violin, my grandfather's desk, and a beloved cherry Biedermeier corner cupboard.

My grandfather's desk was about to be shipped to an antique auction house, when in distress, I relayed to my mother-in-law that this was the only piece my mother requested remain in the family, and was bequeathed to my brother. She quickly gave me the $500 so I could buy it back. At the time my brother and I were estranged, and the manager of the Family Ties geriatric business I had hired to assist me, contacted my brother with the funds for him. He had declined wanting the desk opting for the money, which allowed him to visit his mother one last time.

The weeks of preparing the house for sale were daunting. I was fortunate to have the help of a young woman with whom my mother had become good friends. When Mom suffered her first stroke and the young woman and I were at the hospital, I confessed to her that I had been jealous of her. I heard wonderful things about her, everything I had myself yearned to hear from my mother. We bonded and she spent countless hours assisting me. Left in the now vacant house were many oak pieces of furniture Mom had accumulated over the years. My sweet new friend was setting up house-keeping, and she became the owner of these as a repayment.

The house was finally purchased by a university couple that were Jewish. After the sale, we too became friends, and I could not help thinking how strange life turns out to be. Mom had strongly defended Jews in Germany, and now her beloved home would be appreciated by this couple. Serendipity at its best!

The Family Ties manager insisted I tell Mom that her house was sold, but I feared this like a child, refusing to bring up the subject with her. Finally, she and I sat down with her explaining she'd be given the best care possible, but it would take a lot of money, and for that her house had to be sold. At that moment Mom's face, that previously held no emotion, was contorted in an awful pained way. I sobbingly embraced her in the wheelchair. She sighed saying, "It's OK." Until then she had not spoken as the last stroke had taken her speech, and I immediately understood why I had to have this talk. It absolved me of guilt.

In the final days of emptying the house my husband, his parents, our daughters, his sister and brother-in-law, and their three children spent an entire day throwing out accumulated junk. We hired a dump truck that quickly filled. I realized again why she could never have moved on, of her own volition, she was just too weighed down.

The new millennium was approaching. My husband and I both worked at the crossroads of the community, his church at one end of the main intersection and my library at the other end. We both enjoyed being part of our multi-cultural community. Both of us joined active community groups. An enthusiastic group of residents was forming to celebrate the new millennium. I joined as a promoter and planner of our towns First Night event to ring in the new century. Bumper stickers and entry buttons featured the designs of high school students for the Celebration 2000 event.

Despite lingering possibilities of a Y2K world-wide computer shut-down, it was a festive occasion. As the clock ticked away the final hours of 1999, everyone moved from their various activities to the football field to see the big sports clock turn midnight. It was a misty night making it almost magical when the balloons were released and the high school band played Auld Lang Syne. Returning home that evening, I smiled to myself as I surveyed the canned goods, paper products, and water jugs I had stock-piled in the event the dire predictions occurred, but the world moved smoothly into the year 2000.

Our daughters had off for President's Day week in February, and since the world had not ended, we took our last big trip with them. Our older daughter had shown interest and ability in art, portraits being her specialty. As a graduation present to both our daughters we traveled to Rome and Florence. It was one of our best trips, touring the glorious plazas and galleries, and saw Pope John Paul II in one of his final appearances.

Mom's health was rapidly failing. On the evening of March 31, I received a call that the end was near. I attended church the following morn-ing asking the congregation for emotional support and prayers, and left directly from there for the two- and half-hour drive to the nursing home. I quickly went to her room and to my horror found a stripped bed, and like a child I ran into the hall asking where my mother was. She had died in the morning hours of April 1, and we'd missed the notifying phone call while driving there.

Her wish was to be buried in Germany, however, having been denied that by her hometown cemetery association I had to come up with a plan B. We visited the new owners of her home, and they agreed to her ashes being buried at the edge of the property. It was a private ceremony with the four of us, a friend and her daughter, and we marked the gravesite with a small engraved bronze plaque. As I poured her ashes into the opening my husband had dug, small metal buttons of the housecoat she always wore tumbled out as we said our final goodbye.

During a memorial luncheon with friends at a German restaurant in Bellefonte, I spoke on what I was most grateful for that my mom had taught me:

1. *Small gifts retain a friendship. "Kleine Geschenke erhalten die freundschaft."*
2. *Everything has a solution…think calmly and it will come to you.*
3. *Ask, it doesn't cost anything.*
4. *Do things well, if you are going to do it. "Wenn schon, den schon."*
5. *Trying beats studying. "Probieren geht uber studieren."*
6. *Be non-judgmental. "Great spirit, grant that I may not criticize my neighbor until I have walked one mile in his moccasins."*
7. *To live with God is to see him in all things. "Wer mit Gott lebt, erkennt ihn in allen Dinge."*
8. *Choose your friends wisely. "Von jedem Menchen der Dir in Dein Leben tritt, nimmst Du am Saum ein Staubchen mit. She told me that whoever I associated with some trace would remain on me. As a child I wondered where this was?*
9. *Always be truthful. "Es ist nicht so fein gesponen es kommt an dass Leicht der Sonne." Nothing is so subtle that it will not come to light.*

I had set aside some of the ashes, and kept them in a container in her father's desk, until returning to Germany eight years later where we scattered them at the family grave. This chapter of my life was over. Perhaps unknowingly, Mom, had helped shape me into the person I would become. I had learned persistence, patience, and courtesy. Though my life had been bittersweet, I always felt something better awaited me. In my search for normality and happiness, I discovered that everything has a purpose.

> *To everything there is a season,*
> *And a time for every purpose under heaven:*
> *A time to be born, a time to die;*
> *A time to plant, and a time to pluck up what is planted;*
> *A time to hurt, and a time to heal;*
> *A time to break down, and a time to build up;*
> *A time to weep, and a time to laugh;*
> *A time to mourn, and a time to dance.*

I continued my community work with involved residents for the town's Annual Youth Appreciation Week. Our artist daughter designed the logo for the placemats used at restaurants to promote the week's activities, and the event sponsors. Posters around town featured the week long activities: spelling bee, essay contest, youth forum, library activities, and multi-cultural day. The culminating event was a Family Fun Day with pony rides, petting zoo, inflatables, and sidewalk chalk at the town's spacious Oval. The day ended with a big screen movie on the lawn.

Our older daughter had begun her college search. We told our girls that, with our modest means, we would pay for a public university provided their chosen fields led to a job after graduation. Both took this seriously, and one became a nurse and the other a teacher.

The tragedy of September 11, 2001 struck. Seven residents of our community died in the collapse of the World Trade Towers that claimed the life of three thousand people that fateful day of the terrorist attacks on our country. My husband and I had visited the Windows of the World restaurant that July to celebrate our wedding anniversary. The staff was considerate and gracious, it was hard for us think they too were gone.

It was also a time to grieve and honor lost members of our community. My husband worked with other clergy in interfaith seminars, services, and counseling for family and friends of the departed. I joined a planning committee for a permanent living memorial garden. The garden is enjoyed by many as a place of reflection, with a sun dial made from steel beams of the Trade Towers, and the exact time the planes hit inscribed on the dial. A capsule containing charred ashes of the towers lay buried beneath the sun dial.

Following the tragedy, it was apparent that drum beats of war were stirring. In support of peaceful solutions, we attended peace vigils in neighboring towns. On the coldest day of winter, we took the Path train to Manhattan joining millions worldwide in the run-up to the Iraq War. Having come from a pacifist tradition, my husband began thinking about doing something besides that of a local pastor. It seemed we were heading toward a crisis of cultures, and that wider perspectives were sorely needed.

We were again going on a retreat, this time to the Long Island Sound in Connecticut, where we could think calmly and clearly. We were on our way when our older daughter called to say she was moving in with a girl-friend for her final semester. She had spent two years attending Seton Hall University and living at home. Her final semester was paid for by the hospital she would work for, a welcomed financial relief. We began to realize this might be a sign to reinvent ourselves and move on.

That summer my husband gave the customary time to the board of the church of our decision to relocate to Pennsylvania. We would stay to help with the Annual Fall Festival held every year in early October. Preparations started a week in advance as people dropped off donated items, what we fondly called attic treasures. My responsibility, since our arrival, was the Toys & Games table. Our daughters were then six and eight years old. Located conveniently at the main intersection of town the Fall Festival became well known. To curtail haggling, each table had a sign

"Thank you for not bargaining, prices are already low and proceeds go to the church."

Ladies of the church purchased red aprons with pockets making helpers easily identified. During later years we had a café serving beverages, hot dogs, and hamburgers with homemade relish. Colorful umbrellas and table-clothed card tables lined the parking lot. Banners inviting everyone were displayed well in advance of the date. Only once in fourteen years did we have to move everything into our big hall due to a rainstorm. We would not be there, however, for the Annual Spaghetti dinner night, complete with tuxedoed maître d, strolling violin player, and colorful waxed wine candle bottles on red and white checked table cloths.

Then came the goodbye dinner party along with the shedding of tears. At each location I'd spend weeks wiping tears away for I knew that once gone we could never go back in the same way. In each congregation we retained a few close friends, often people that had joined during our tenure. Packing was completed and the Atlas moving van was in our driveway, when one of our parishioner's pulled up to say a farewell thanking us for being there for them. All of this reminded me of my husband's first sermon at each congregation entitled "The Light is On," meaning someone was now there for the highs and low of their lives. My emotions got the best of me knowing the light would be off. I had enjoyed my role as a minister's wife, but was ready to move on.

16. FAREWELLS

As part of our farewell, we were invited to a Town Hall meeting during which my husband and I were presented a plaque by the Mayor and Town Council. It proclaimed October 10th to be known as Barbara and David Long Day because of our efforts, fellowship, and friendship. It was a recognition from a community that welcomed and appreciated us.

WHEREAS Barbara has been a tireless and selfless volunteer always lending involvement and leadership to many community-wide events and organizations such as Youth Appreciation Week, Celebration 2000, the opening of the new Senior & Community Center, the 9-11 Living Memorial Garden, and president of the Friends of the Library. Always willing to lend encouragement, a smile and a helping hand. Barbara is the epitome of "gracious giving," and

WHEREAS David has been a spiritual leader always willing to deliver words of comfort, sharing, warmth, and wisdom at many town-wide events such as the annual Re-organization of the Township Council, Memorial Day Services, Veterans services, the commemorations of 9-11, Martin Luther King Day, and community Thanksgiving Day services.

Our fourteen years in New Jersey were enjoyable years, both professionally and personally. One of the highlights of our week was a standing invitation to a friend's home for dinner along with other like-minded progressive and liberal friends. A favorite yearly event was the evening in spring to celebrate the magnolia tree blossoms with this family. Twice a year our friend turned her basement and garden into an evening of Satsang Satsang is Sanskrit, for a group of spiritual seekers. Occasionally a guru from The Temple of Peace in upstate New Yok would be invited too. We were increasingly interested of other traditions that sought peace and respect for all humanity. We sometimes hosted drumming circles on our backyard, much to the chagrin of our teenage daughters who peered out the windows.

While our older daughter attended West Chester University her first year, we visited her, and fell in love with the area. It was near Philadelphia, the birthplace of democracy and our nation, with many historical traditions and sites. All this had deep meaning for myself and my husband. The Brandywine Valley was lovely, with the Andrew Wyeth Art Gallery, and the beautiful Longwood Gardens.

After several trips to West Chester we found charming Audubon, a small townhouse community on the side of a hill surrounded by beautiful trees. I had told our realtor that we wanted to live in a unique and liberal community. He laughed as he told us that he was the only liberal progressive in his sales force, and that it was a conservative area. Little did we know that three years later this was about to change when the county and state chose Barack Obama as President.

We were about to sign the contract, when I had an uneasy feeling, and asked if we could resume later that afternoon. Returning to the community we quickly realized we could not see ourselves in that particular townhouse, it was close to a busy road and creek. In a phone call to the realtor we were asked to meet at another recently vacated unit in the same complex. The minute we stepped across the threshold we knew it was the perfect home for us. A phone call followed, we were the new owners, and exactly on my birthday! Our new life was beckoning but most of all, this was our house, as a popular song states:

I'll light the fire
You put the flowers in the vase that you bought today
Staring at the fire for hours and hours while I listen to you
Play your love songs all night long for me, only for me

Now everything is easy because of you
Our house is a very, very, very fine house with two cats in the yard
Life used to be so hard
Now everything is easy because of you
I'll light the fire while you place the flowers in the vase that you
bought today

We now had a cat, a fireplace, and usually a vase of flowers. It was our very own first home with three floors, fireplace, two decks, and a patio outside my husband's study. One of the first gifts we received from a former parishioner couple was an intercom system, which we used continuously. The couple had recalled a sermon my husband gave in which he gently reminded us to avoid yelling to one another from room to room. What was surprising to me was that these folks remembered. I often felt lasting impressions are left with people in the course of Sunday morning messages.

We were relocating, yet neither of us had jobs. A church member surprised us with a sizable check, but the funds soon ran out. While still working at the library, and feeling particularly melancholic that day, a call came from the sales representative of World Book wanting to speak to our library director. We were an account in her territory, and after perfunctory greetings, I asked where her sales manager was located. To my amazement his office was only forty minutes away from our new West Chester home. It was a breakthrough serendipitous moment, and I proceeded to contact him.

During my phone call with this manager, he indicated they didn't have any territory for me, to which I began reciting the awards I'd received during my earlier years with World Book. I gave him the name of the retired president of the company who knew me during my first tenure. Just like the actress Julia Roberts replied in one of her movies, I told him he was making a "Big Mistake!" Not long afterward he called back saying that four counties of schools and libraries would be assigned to me. By the time I retired after fourteen years I had thirteen counties including Philadelphia.

I planned on starting in January allowing time to settle into our new home. However, paperwork was delayed by the company until mid-January when the necessary signatures were secured. By the summer sales conference my name tag had winning ribbons attached. I had met assigned quotas and was looking forward to a trip for two to Alaska, all expenses paid including airfare.

Close to the end of the year I noticed my name was not listed as in the running, even though I had already met my yearly quota. I was informed that the contest was only for those who had joined the company as of January 1. Of course, I never saw that written anywhere, and was not informed of this when I signed up. Being an optimist, I felt certain they'd see I had signed in November, and was just waiting for the president's signature. Granted, there was a change in leadership that November. I wrote letters of disappointment, but in the end, I did not get to go. I was so discouraged that my husband planned a cruise to the Caribbean for the two of us the following spring.

I knew the company felt some remorse in their decision because at the next summer sales conference I won the first "Rookie of the Year" award. Plus, the rules as to who could go on these company trips had also changed. Now anyone who made their yearly quota was invited. The company's explanation was if I had won, it would have meant another person would not have. Some solace.

After all expense paid trips to Hawaii, Los Cabos, and Cancun, I came perilously close to again not being awarded a trip. This time I didn't remain silent, even used the dreaded word "discrimination," and I was awarded the trip as a "wild card" winner. It didn't matter what they called it; we were going on the cruise! I had learned over a lifetime, often the hard way, to stand up for what was right.

Upon moving to West Chester our search began for a spiritual community. It was clear that we were seeking an inclusive and progressive community. We attended various Quaker Meetings, but we knew that their services were quite different from what we were used too. During his growing years my husband's best friends had been Unitarian or Jewish, so we started to explore Unitarian Universalists. Having met some of the Unitarian members at peace vigils we knew this was a real possibility. The town had become a hub of social justice and political activism, and protests were held every Saturday at the main intersection.

Soon after we started attending the local Unitarian congregation, and readings at a Sunday service included world religions and progressive ideas, my husband looked at me, and whispered "I'm in" to which I replied "Me too." We were also impressed by the Seven Principles of Unitarian Universalism:

> *1st Principle: The inherent worth and dignity of every person;*
>
> *2nd Principle: Justice, equity and compassion in human relations;*
>
> *3rd Principle: Acceptance of one another and encouragement to spiritual growth in our congregations;*
>
> *4th Principle: A free and responsible search for truth and meaning;*
>
> *5th Principle: The right of conscience and the use of the democratic process within our congregations and in society at large;*
>
> *6th Principle: The goal of world community with peace, liberty, and justice for all;*
>
> *7th Principle: Respect for the interdependent web of all existence of which we are a part.*

Not long after joining I was asked to become a Membership Committee person, of which I later became chairperson. It was apparent I enjoyed meeting and greeting new people. My husband led small groups and spoke during summer months while the minister was away. I created a greeter team, and meetings followed emphasizing customer service skills. We were moving on, as our new-found place gave us fresh ideas and approaches to life.

Unitarian Universalism affirms the Seven Principles, which they try to live out in the Living Traditions of wisdom and spirituality, drawn from sources as diverse as science, literature, scripture, and personal experience.

> *Direct experience of that transcending mystery and wonder, affirmed in all cultures, which moves us to a renewal of the spirit and an openness to the forces which create and uphold life;*
>
> *Words and deeds of prophetic women and men which challenge us to confront powers and structures of evil with justice, compassion, and the transforming power of love;*
>
> *Wisdom from the world's religions which inspires us in our ethical and spiritual life;*
>
> *Jewish and Christian teachings which call us to respond to God's love by loving our neighbors as ourselves;*
>
> *Humanist teachings which counsel us to heed the guidance of reason and the results of science, and warn us against idolatries of the mind and spirit;*
>
> *Spiritual teachings of Earth-centered traditions which celebrate the sacred circle of life and instruct us to live in harmony with the rhythms of nature.*

Thomas Jefferson closely aligned to Unitarianism, and thought someday all Americans would become Unitarian. Though we're far from that goal, Unitarians keep moving forward. Famous Unitarians include four of the first five American Presidents, John Adams, Thomas Jefferson, James Madison, and John Quincy Adams.

We had arrived where we wanted to be, emotionally and spiritually. The community embraced us for who we were, not what we were supposed to be. I was successful in my work, one year earning the highest achievement award in the company. My husband was doing what he loved, teaching young people at a local college in the field of Humanities and World Religions. As a peace activist he became a frequent writer in blogs and papers across the country, including the New York Times and Newsweek. Due to subsequent events, we found ourselves drawn to new progressive causes, and became part of a group called "Defenders of Democracy."

While planning a trip to Germany to return my mother's ashes, I made a phone call to the son of my father's brother. I had never met him. My brother had suggested I contact him and gave me his name. I will be forever grateful to my brother for this, and consider it a priceless gift. In the internet directory this cousin's name was the only one listed in the area. I made a phone call, and asked if he was interested in meeting me after so many years, and he replied "of course." I was overjoyed! His two siblings and he were going on a retreat the following weekend where he would share the news about me. I received photos of the three, and was told where to meet at the train station, after we left Berlin heading to the Rhine Valley. It was an amazing afternoon with the cousins, their children, and grandchildren.

The following year we returned to Germany for a reunion. My cousins rented a guest farm for all twenty-one of us. Meals were arranged, and children played with animals on the farm, while the men congregated in the steam room to philosophize about the state of the world. I embraced my new family, and deep relationships formed. One cousin had surprisingly visited my mother's mother, even after my parent's divorce. Another cousin and her husband had lived in Washington DC for three years as a German ambassador. It was yet another needless misfortune to not know my extended family due to my mother's hostility to my father and his family.

More visits followed, including another pilgrimage to my father's grave. There we noticed that a third person was buried in the small plot, and wondered who this was. Through this mystery we discovered my father's godchild. He had visited the grave a month after our visit, and found my note tucked next to the headstone. He knew little about me other than my name. The godson then inquired with the cemetery caretakers about who the third person was, as I did also. The official there sent a letter to me asking that I contact this godson. I made a phone call to Berlin, and immediately felt a bond with him and his family. The mystery remained unsolved as to why the wife of my father's lawyer was buried next to my father and his second wife

On our first visit in Berlin as an extended family, my cousins and their spouses, along with my husband and I, met with the godson and his young family. Reminisces were shared over a dinner at a typical German restaurant in the former East Berlin. My dreams of reconnecting with my father through the people who knew him best were coming true. . My father's godson attributed much of his success as a film producer to my father's influence. He and his brother had spent summers vacationing in the Bavarian Alps with my father. The two observed how diligently, calmly, and carefully my father worked on his research papers. What I yearned and ached for over decades was a reality for these young boys, and for my father the joy of being with children.

Two years later we visited again with this couple on the day of the terrorist attack in Berlin, when a truck deliberately drove into the Christmas Market next to Kaiser Wilhelm Church. Eleven people lost their lives and fifty-six were injured. We had just left another Christmas Market in the trendy eastern section of the city. As the newscasts were reporting what had happened, we were seated in at a cozy restaurant enjoying dinner. My cousin in Hamburg called, frantically asking where we were. The next day Instead of visiting places of interest, we somberly took a cab to the train stain. The modernistic station swarmed with armed police. We breathed a sigh of relief when we arrived safely at my cousin's home.

Meanwhile in the States, our daughter and son-in-law discovered an official file containing sixty pages about my father available under the Freedom of Information Act, a law giving the right to obtain personal information. It concerned his request and the governments review of him to become a permanent resident of the United States,

What was evident was the thoroughness of the report, and my father's desire to assimilate to the American way of life. The authorities were suspicious, and rightly so, of any scientist who had at one time worked under Nazi times. The investigation went back to his youth, friends, schooling, jobs in Germany, and his work at Wright Patterson. My mother, brother, and I were listed as his top priority to come to America. The file contained not only his personal traits, and family history but also his relations to work and government. The report concluded he had been a great asset to the United States, and was cleared of any suspicions.

This significant file arrived the day my brother passed away in the early hours of a January morning. Having been six years older than myself, and in contact with my father throughout their lives, he knew much more about my father and who he really was. I was happy to have these details of my father's past, yet I felt wistful, too, thinking of all the people who knew my father better than I did. Each fact as well as each story shared was a gift. Why did I miss not knowing this intelligent, gentle and well-liked man?

In writing this story, it wasn't my intention to have the closing section about my brother, however, after his death it seemed the right thing to do. I began writing this memoir at the seashore listening to the breaking waves of the Atlantic Ocean, when my cell phone rang. It was the call I received each year from the Social Security Administration concerning my brother's ability to retain his benefits. I answered the questions that I knew by heart:

1. *Is your brother married? No.*
2. *Does he have children? No.*
3. *Does he have a car? No.*
4. *Does he have a job? No.*
5. *Does he own a home? No*
6. *Does he own property? No*

7. Does he have a savings account? No

8. Does he have a pension? N

9. Does he have a 401K? No

10. Does he have family? Yes, I am his only sibling.

My brother had many wonderful qualities, good looks, intelligence, gentleness, wit, and charm. His life proved the inverse of the saying: *Sticks and stones may break my bones, but words will never hurt me.* Because of hurts, he was not able to move on, so much damage had taken place. As much as I and others tried to help, he remained broken. The realization I had, at twelve years old, that he would not have a happy life had come true. I was comforted by the quote: *Grief is like the ocean, it comes in waves, ebbing and flowing. Sometimes the water is calm, and sometimes it is overwhelming. All we can do is learn to swim.* I had tried to do just that!

I spoke with my brother by phone on what was the last day of his life. When I asked how he was doing, I think he wanted to tell me he was dying, but all he said, "Very bad." I had become so used to his complaining; I gave a pep talk about how poorly people are treated today. He was aware enough to acknowledge that, but when it was time to say goodbye, he said nothing, and the call ended. My brother had spent the last fifteen years of his life in an assisted living facility in Florida, with caring helpers and fellow residents, all good friends. While hospitalized, a resident called him twice a day. He was the last person to speak to him.

While making funeral arrangements, I again answered many questions, this time for his death certificate. What was his profession? I was silent as I pondered how to answer. Upon my hesitation the official asked "Where had he been employed?" I answered, Lawrence Livermore Laboratory. It was the only place I knew that he was officially an employee. He replied, so he was a nuclear physicist? I answered quietly yes; he was. I thought to myself how finally in death he was being recognized. When friends asked me how I was doing, I told them I missed what could have been. I choked up when I read the words on a sympathy card I received:

"A brother is someone who gives you lots to remember, to laugh about, to be grateful for, and to love. Hope you can smile even through the tears, when you think about how lucky you were to have him for a brother, and all he meant to you now and always."

We didn't have this kind of brother and sister relationship. I had made my choice as a young girl to refuse contact with our father. My brother continued his relationship with him as he always yearned to be a scientist, like his father. Because of this there was unnecessary distance between us. I wish to honor my brother for who he was, and also what happened to him. I know he was proud of me, especially during the last decade plus years of his life. With each death, first my father, then my mother, and lastly my brother, I felt the deep ache of loss about what might have been. Family has been important to me, never to be taken for granted.

I am indebted to Gulf Coast Jewish Family Services who secured his assisted living facility. It was MLK day when I made phone calls for help, sensing he was not well. Many agencies were either closed or unavailable to help. JFCS immediately offered their assistance. When they visited him, it was apparent that he had acute renal failure, and arranged for his hospitalization. The counselor comforted me by saying "If it was my brother, I would choose the home on Fourth Street once he's discharged from the hospital."

My husband and I flew to Florida in late spring after his death, the time for our annual visit around his birthday. Upon our arrival at the group home the manager set his urn on the front seat of our car, next to a bag of chocolate chip cookies, his favorite. On the drive back to our hotel, listening to his generation's music on the radio, I touched the urn, and said I was here to take him home.

A white van pulled up to the spot where my brother and I had spent many hours watching the ocean waves. Caregivers and residents gathered, and I thanked them for their care and dedication. His roommate was present despite having said it would be hard for him to come. During the gathering I put a page of an essay he had written as a young man in the urn. In the writing he had expressed gratitude for having been able to travel noting the words of a German folksong, *when God wishes to show someone favor, he sends him into the wide world.* Each resident had written a thought about my brother on a slip of paper which we added to the urn while the folksong played in the background.

For a lasting memorial at the group home, my husband and I purchased a park bench including a plaque with his name, and the years he spent there. In a dream, a few days after his death, my brother came to me, requesting that the bench face west, the direction of his beloved ocean, as now it does. He has returned several more times in my dreams, now always happy and healthy.

A poem written by our then third grade daughter, captured what happened in my and my brother's life. Her natural feelings come through, something we were not allowed to show in our growing years.

If I had a world, my world would have sad, but no mad.
I would see only good, that would make a difference in my world.
With sadness, with tears, but no fears, for this is my world.
When you play, do not say bad words, for that is forbidden in my world.
For my world would have light and brightness, and no fights, not in
my world.

This young woman went on to become a registered nurse and Family Nurse Practitioner. She married a business manager at a firm in New York City, have two daughters, and reside in northern New Jersey.

Our younger daughter became a teacher, and proprietor of a preschool children's center. Her creed there is: *We know that every child is unique and has their own special interests and needs. Our goal is to encourage the love of learning and exploration of the world around them while providing a safe, stimulating, and nurturing environment.* She is married to a businessman who manages his own start-up company. They have three daughters, and live near the ocean in Massachusetts.

Our tranquil life includes our daughters, son-in-law's, and five grand-daughters. We know life has both bitter and sweet experiences, and they both make us who we are. In our home is a hymnbook with the words of a song, beloved in our family:

My life flows on in endless song
above earth's lamentation.
I hear the real, thought far off hymn
That hails the new creation
Above the tumult and the strife,
I hear the music ringing;
It sounds an echo in my soul
How can I keep from singing!

POSTSCRIPT

Listening to the hypnotic roar of the ocean waves crashing on to the shore, my husband and I began and finished writing this memoir. The immensity and constancy of the sea brought up many forgotten memories, and helped me get back to me. A popular song I loved to sing in childhood was "Que Sera, Sera." The lyrics became kind of a mantra for me.

Que sera, sera,
Whatever will be, will be,
The future's not ours to see
Que sera, sera,
What will be, will be.

The future is not ours to see, but choices matter, as do the words we say, and the things we do. I still believe *what will be will be,* but also that *God gives every bird its food, but doesn't throw it into the nest.* Throughout the years I believed if I kept going, I'd become stronger and wiser. In the words of Albert Einstein: *Life is like riding a bicycle. To keep your balance, you must keep moving.*

In the classic movie "It's A Wonderful Life," the Angel Clarence shows George Bailey that he really had a wonderful life. In my case, the first half of life was unnecessarily hard, yet thankfully something better awaited. A saying that helped, and still helps me is, *keep it simple, keep it true, keep it real.*

At an early age I learned to detach from an unhappy life, and later as I realized I was not responsible for others' behavior. Because of this I managed, most of the time, to not let circumstances take over. Mom had tried to do the best that she was capable of doing. Yet children of a dysfunctional home, like mine, will never be completely spared from side effects. In my case, I still suffer from insomnia that started during the scary nights when my mother's anxieties got the best of her. Still, I was fortunate I was not denied a career despite all that had happened.

Those affected by mental illness, as well as those around them, tragically suffer. Mental illness is like any other disease, in that both require medication. What is lost through the years, without professional help, is difficult to recover. Though my mother never made apologies, I know she suffered. I often wonder if my dad's life was cut short due to grief and heartache. Divorce is a devastating time for everyone, especially children. Estrangement from a parent almost always is heartbreaking. I hope that my story shows the tragic consequences when issues go unresolved.

A framed copy of "The Guest House" by the Sufi Mystic Rumi hangs on a wall in our home. It is a reminder not to resist the thoughts and emotions that flow through us, but to meet them with courage and respect. Rumi's poem relates how the entirety of human experience is valuable.

> *Being human is like a guest house,*
> *Every morning a new arrival.*
> *Some momentary awareness comes*
> *As an unexpected visitor.*
>
> *Welcome and entertain them all!*
> *Even if they're a crowd of sorrows*
> *who violently sweep your house*
> *empty of its furniture,*
> *still treat each guest honorably.*
> *He may be clearing you out*
> *for some new delight.*
>
> *Be grateful for whoever comes,*

because each has been sent
as a guide from beyond.

This book is for all who have struggled, like my father, my mother, my brother, and myself. These reflections are bittersweet memories of the best and worst in human nature. In times of turmoil there is always a way out. Professionals, family, and friends are there to help. I've had many guides who showed me what is most important in life.

I could not have accomplished writing this memoir without the help of my beloved husband and editor, from the beginning he felt it was a story worth telling. My daughters, relatives, and friends gave input and support. Thanks to everyone who encouraged me; may this book be an encouragement to others.

ABOUT THE AUTHOR

Barbara Hussmann Long was born in Bad Homburg, Germany, and grew up near State College, Pennsylvania. She has two married daughters, five granddaughters, and lives with her husband on the Long Island Sound.

She worked in sales, management, and marketing and is involved in community and civic projects. She can be found on Facebook and at Bittersweetmemories.net.